I NEED A FRIEND

I NEED A FRIEND

*An innovative look At The Treatment of
Children's Anxiety Disorders Using Allies*

Sandra Nelson, MA, NCC

To order additional copies of this book, contact:
Xlibris Corporation
1-888-795-4274
www.Xlibris.com
Orders@Xlibris.com
82456

CONTENTS

"We'll begin with a spin traveling in the world of my creation;
What we'll see will defy explanation;
Come with me and you'll be in a world
Of pure imagination."
Willie Wonka

How did God make mothers? "Magic plus super powers and a lot of stirring".
A second grader

"Mom's have magic. They make you feel better without medicine".
A first grader

Dedication

This book is dedicated to my good friend Rosemary Eberle Peterson, who, along with her oldest daughter Selena, taught me how to deal with Wayward Lions.

ACKNOWLEDGEMENTS

The author wishes to recognize two good friends and cohorts, Peggy Finder Sullivan, MA, NCC and Dr. Catherine Mac Lennan, PhD, NCC for their encouragement and editing assistance that brought this book to life. Thanks also to my own therapist, Dr. Robert Ozwald, for breaking his own rules and letting me raid his library, for being such a good listener and giving sage advice that keeps my boat sailing with an even keel. And last, but not least, my loving husband, Dean, who encourages me to take on whatever task is at hand, who believes in me every day, and who loves me in spite of myself. He is my rock and the wind beneath my wings. He also willingly offered his editing and computer skills that helped guide me through the process of writing a book. Plus he sat with me in the city library for hours as I researched books and took notes while he ran errands finding more books for me to research and take even more notes. He scanned books as possible resources, which saved me an enormous amount of time and energy. Without his help this book would not have come to be.

I would also like to thank my four wonderful sons for teaching me how to be a parent and for continuing to love me every day even through my failures. And who, along with the hundreds of children and numerous families who have been my clients, taught me about being a child. Working with them through all their ups and downs has been a true learning experience that cannot be found in any books.

INTRODUCTION

You may suspect you have a child in your practice, home, classroom or otherwise in your care and this has led you to pick up this book and read it. I have jam packed as much information as I could to help you learn to cope with the child's behavior in an innovative way I have had much success with. That is using friends or "allies" to help the child get back to the way they were before anxiety took control. Allies can be real or imagined. What is most important is the child *believes* this ally has some special power or strength that can help them. So let's explore children's anxieties, how they come to be and most of all what can you do to help. I hope using allies works as well for you as it has for me.

This book is about children's anxieties that are severe enough that the parent(s) seek help, usually from a mental health professional. Children of any age can suffer from anxiety, but this book addresses primarily Anxiety Disorders in pre-school aged children, ages three to five, who can still respond to suggestion and magical thinking. They still believe in Santa Claus, the Tooth Fairy and the Easter Bunny. The treatment recommendations contained in this book are targeted to those therapists, who work with this population, and the parents who live with them, the caregivers who care for them and teachers who teach them.

Although this book focuses on the use of "magical" allies to assist young children to cope with their fears and worries the same way of thinking about treating the problem only using more realistic allies because they are too old to fall for the magic, sometimes, but not always.

Parents, caregivers, teachers and therapists may find helpful information to help cope with and cure anxieties in children of any age. Helping children with the use of allies can be done with any age group, it's just done a bit differently with older children whose heroes have more clearly defined super powers. Using the concept of allies to help children cope with

Anxiety Disorders is simply guided imagery techniques and play therapy with a magical twist.

The ideas described are quite simple and can be used by anyone working closely with children. Although treatment suggestions are directed toward therapists they are easily put into use by anyone. Parents are an integral part of any kind of therapy treatment of their children and particularly so using these treatment recommendations so it is essential they have some understanding of the theory and use of "magical allies" to treat anxiety disorders with their child. Teachers and caregivers can also not only be helpful, but can also become allies, as can parents.

If you have a child who is suffering from severe anxiety and you have reached the point you need to reach out for help then this book should be helpful. And hopefully this book will help to promote an integrated treatment program where all the adults in the child's life are speaking the same language and reading from the same page and all understand what allies are and how they are being used to help the child.

I believe that when we know better, we do better. I believe that information is empowering, therefore, I have included as much information as I could. Some is not directly related to the treatment of Anxiety Disorders but can be helpful in gaining an *accurate* picture of the child who is suffering. With some of this information the child will then be seen and treated in a holistic manner that fits within their world and as they see themselves.

I did not intend to write a dry, theoretical book that would bore the reader to distraction. So I have tried to alternate the more serious information with real stories about real children who have had troubles with fears and anxieties, not all of whom needed mental health help, but were just kids with worries that disrupted the family life somehow. I hope that these stories, sometimes funny, help you, the reader, get a better glimpse into the life of a child who is afraid.

So off we go into the world where children can really use a friend (an ally) to help them conquer their worries and fears. I hope you find some useful information to help you get an *accurate* picture of the child and how they should be treated.

FACING OUR FEARS

Susan's 7-year-old daughter, Kylie, has lots of friends. She plays soccer, swims, and sings in the church choir. She likes to help her teachers and is the first one in class to raise her hand to volunteer. Even her parent's divorce two years ago doesn't seem to have had major repercussions. She merrily, with a big smile on her face, goes to her father's house every other weekend and gets along well with her new step-siblings. To everyone who knows her, she's the model of a well adjusted child.

Except this: When she's at home with Susan at night, she sticks to her like glue. "She's afraid to go anywhere in the house alone, even though we've lived there for four years," Susan says. Routine tasks, like taking out the trash, can become cumbersome. And bedtime rituals take hours. Susan often falls asleep on her own bed with her child after giving up on negotiations to have Kylie go to sleep in the room she shares with her sister. Sleepovers have thus far been out of the question. "Having all the lights on helps, but the fear is still there. This extends to other houses, like her grandparents' and her Dad's as well."

Susan is at the end of her rope. "We read two books that focus more on being afraid of the dark, not specifically about being alone in a room. They might have helped . . . a little. My older daughter had this same fear, but she got over it by the age of 7. Not so far with this child."

Across town, Keri is negotiating with 4-year old Meredith, who is close to tears. She hasn't been willing to use the downstairs bathroom since the toilet flooded six months ago, and she still won't, even though it has long since been repaired. So Keri waits patiently at the foot of the stairs while Meredith heads upstairs to use the bathroom in her room. They're running late, again. Keri hopes the restaurant where they are meeting friends doesn't have automatic flush toilets, or it's going to be a long night.

Meanwhile, Julia's father, Joe, has just returned home with a crying 10-year-old daughter and raw nerves after another failed bicycle outing. Although she's agile and able, Julia refuses to ride her bike across the street. He's walked her bike across every intersection along with his own, and he's tired, frustrated and concerned. "I learned to ride a two-wheeler when I was four years old," he says. "I don't understand why she's so afraid."

Many parents remember their childhood fears-everything from monsters under the bed, big dogs, and swimming, to bigger fears, such as having a parent die or being sick ourselves. But when these fears emerge in their own children and their parenting skills fail them, they don't always know what to do.

"Some fears are easy to empathize with, but this one has been hard for me," admits Susan. "My oldest daughter went through it too but grew out of it by the age of seven." But Kylie shows no signs of recovery from her debilitating fear. Susan goes on to say, "I've been taught that it's important to validate a child's feelings, but there are times that I've lost my patience and said, 'that's enough. Just go to bed.' We both go to bed upset. That doesn't make me feel like a good parent."

Most research and accepted field practices agree that ninety percent of all children between ages 2 and 14 have one specific fear at some point in their lives. Some fears occur in response to an event in the life of the child, but continue long beyond expectations. Some fears simply appear "out of the blue". Some come on gradually and worsen over time while others appear suddenly with no warning. Most often these fears seem completely irrational. They can't be explained away.

There are common fears specific to age groups. From birth to 2 years old, loud noises, strangers and separation from parents are the most prevalent. During the preschool years, common fears include imaginary figures, supernatural beings, the dark, noises, sleeping alone, thunder, and floods. School age children have "more realistic" fears, such as physical injury, health, school performance, death or natural disasters. This book is intended to address those irrational and imaginary fears children develop with or without an apparent cause.

There is a difference between fear and anxiety. Fear is a healthy reaction. Fear is valid, helpful and an immediate response to a dangerous situation. Fear occurs when the danger is happening. Anxiety occurs when the danger "might be" happening.

It is difficult to separate Anxiety Disorders from Attention Deficit Disorders and other mental health Disorders because the behaviors are most often very similar if the child is acting out. But there is the common thread of worries and fears that lead to the suspected existence of an Anxiety Disorder. I will discuss this later in the chapter on diagnoses.

Anxiety gets in the way or distracts children from their ability to soothe themselves. It robs them of their creativity. They tend to give up too quickly and they don't recognize their own successes. Anxious children have difficulty feeling safe even when they are, in reality, safe. The problem lies in the "*what if*" belief that whatever is causing their anxiety can happen again or is "*really real*".

Although only about 1 in 100 children are diagnosed with Anxiety Disorder, it remains the most prevalent disorder in children and adolescents under the age of 16. There are a number of factors that can contribute to anxiety including temperament, parent-infant attachment, having a parent with a mental illness and differing parenting styles.

Children need enough structure in their lives to feel secure. If parents are too laissez-faire, then the child lacks the feeling of security. If, in their mind, no one is in control, then they will attempt to take over the parenting role. Because they are children, they will fail and feel inadequate and subsequently, anxious. However, even when parents do set limits and guidelines, children can still develop irrational fears that can strain an otherwise orderly parent-child relationship. Parents attempt to soothe and calm their child using all the parenting "tricks of the trade", but to no avail. They try time and time again to offer calm and comfort. Parents try to become an anchor for their child by staying calm themselves, speaking in soft reassuring tones and offering physical comfort such as a reassuring touch. Sometimes, even though they give it their best, it doesn't always work.

Parents want to reflect to their children they are capable of overcoming their fears and to do things even if they are scary. For example, if a child is afraid to cross the street on her bike, as in the case of Joe and Julia, practicing using proper safety precautions and encouraging her to try again (once she is calm), while staying close by is a perfectly normal parental reaction. When it continues to fail over time, it becomes a problem that usually brings the parent and child into the office of a treatment provider. It is just this sort of problem this book is designed to address.

This book is designed to assist practitioners in the field of children's mental health to use creative methods to reach a correct diagnosis and to teach parents to use creative ideas to address their child's fears. The focus of this book is on children of preschool age, from 2 to 6, who can still respond to the use of magical thinking. However, it can also be used with children of any age by using a little creative thinking. Since not all children are not referred to a therapist it falls to the parents, caregivers and teachers to assist the child.

Usually, by the time the parent and child reach the office of a mental health provider, they are both at their wits end and the relationship is in jeopardy. It is important, therefore, to try and relieve the pressure as soon as possible. Hopefully, this book will help the helpers achieve such a goal using creativity and magic as effective tools.

IN THE BEGINNING

In the beginning a child is born into a world with the capability to learn new information, given the assumption there is no organic defect to prevent normal learning. The world is a wonderful place, full of sounds, colors, faces, creatures and movement and those are only the tip of the iceberg. If you watch an infant for a few minutes you will notice their eyes rarely stop moving. Their eyes are the gateway to the world of information. Infants rely on all their senses to assimilate all of the new and wondrous things in their environment. As you observe this baby, suddenly it stops moving. Its eyes are fixed on an object. Their breathing slows down. Their eyes widen. Their cranial neurons are firing a mile a minute. What is this new thing? And then the magic begins.

During infancy and throughout toddlerhood children use all of their senses to accumulate knowledge of the world around them. They begin to make decisions about their world. They use their eyes to see new things. They rely on taste, putting everything within reach in their mouths. They make a decision; does it taste good or does it taste awful? They rely on touch, usually preferring soft things. Things which feel good. They rely on hearing. They enjoy soft soothing sounds. Loud sounds startle them. They make hundreds of decisions about their world every day; perhaps every hour. They are deciding what they like and what they do not. They are thinking. The influx of new information is constant. Everything that enters into their world via all of their senses is new and wondrous. Adults have to consciously stop and smell the roses, but young children stop to smell, taste, touch and listen to everything including the roses. The rapid influx of information would overwhelm an adult, and sometimes overwhelms the child as well, but not as often. Young children are like sponges, soaking up every ounce of information existing in or entering their space. They are naturally curious.

Children are mostly attracted to other people, naturally preferring the human face from birth. At birth a baby is capable of recognizing the sound of their mother's voice and her smell. They know the beat of her heart. They have been listening to sounds in utero. Early on they begin making decisions about the people in their life. Assuming the world is a safe place the infant will begin to express their thinking about the faces they see. Some children are outgoing and happy to explore each new face. Others are shy and are often frightened by new faces. They are making decisions with each new face.

By the time a child reaches toddlerhood they normally have learned to communicate with the other people in their world and they begin to express their decisions using words and symbols to make their opinions known. Their world has gotten much larger and contains even more new and wondrous things and beings. It is a magical place full of colors, sounds, tastes, movement and touches. They are increasingly curious and begin to question their environment.

About the age of 3 children begin to develop imagination. The ability to create images in their brain based on the information they have assimilated. It is quite common, and normal, to observe a toddler talking when no one is there. Perhaps they have created an imaginary friend. Perhaps they are learning to pretend. Young children love to play in the world of pretend. It is at this developmental stage that magical thinking begins.

Most magical thinking is fun for both the child and their parents or other people in their life. However, sometimes the magical thinking creates a problem. There is a lion living under the sofa! There are monsters in my closet! There are bad things in the dark! And thus the child makes decisions based on these imaginary thoughts. I can't sit on the sofa! I can't sleep in my bed! I can't sleep without a light on!

Often times the parents will talk about the problems with grandparents, aunts and uncles, their minister or their neighbors in an effort to resolve the child's fears. And sometimes the problems become serious enough for the parent to seek help from a professional: their pediatrician, family doctor, minister, or a children's mental health specialist or psychiatrist. It is at this point you, as a therapist, will come in contact with the parent and child. Or as a parent, caregiver or teacher you will begin to give some serious thought as how to best help the child and hopefully you all will find some helpful information in this book.

If a child's fears are creating significant distress or impairment in social, academic or other important areas of the child's life, or if parents are frustrated to the point that it is negatively impacting the parent-child relationship, this is the time they seek help.

Untreated anxiety leaves children with an increased risk of developing peer relationship difficulties, academic failure and could lead ultimately to depression or substance abuse. Early intervention at the onset of the anxiety is crucial to the success of treatment goals.

HAVING AN ANXIOUS CHILD

So your child is having some problems with being afraid of something, either real or imagined and it is seriously disrupting your life. You are probably losing sleep, having to take the extra time to deal with a "meltdown" usually at an inopportune time, like when you are late for an appointment or in the middle of the grocery store. Your life, and that of your family is being disrupted. A lot. And you are feeling frustrated, and at times, angry, that nothing you try seems to work. You feel like a failure or a bad parent. Worse yet your child may feel like a failure as well or that they're a bad kid.

There is a stigma about reaching out to mental health providers. You are afraid people will think your child is "crazy". This stigma has improved greatly, but it is still remaining in the thinking of some. It is difficult to ask your health care providers for help because you already feel like a failure and having to ask for help just reinforces that feeling.

Sometimes other family members and friends are less than understanding. They think your child will just get over it. They may think your child simply needs more discipline.

Nothing can be further from the truth. Your child is truly afraid even though their fears may stem from something imaginary and their fear may seem totally irrational. Anxiety that seriously disrupts your lives needs to be addressed and you need help to get through this difficult time. Research has shown that children's serious anxieties, if left untreated, can cause further problems down the road. Your child is reaching out for help and you are just the person to get it for them. First, though, it is helpful to understand some facts about children's anxieties.

Children's anxieties develop in a number of ways and display a variety of behaviors in response to their irrational fears. In order to treat their problems you must first have an *accurate* diagnosis of what kinds of anxieties your child is experiencing, and that is generally done by your health care provider or mental health specialist once you have decided it is time to seek professional help. In order to determine a diagnosis a book called the Diagnostic and Statistical Manual, fourth edition (DSM IV) is commonly used which is a book that specifically lists a series of behaviors and how they occurred to determine which kind of anxiety disorder best fits your child. More information on this procedure is offered later on in the book. It's a question of which slot does your child fit into? To greatly simplify this process, is your child raspberry or strawberry jam? Or perhaps they're not jam at all, but ketchup.

This professional may ask you to fill out any number of questionnaires and they will ask you a lot of questions about how your child reacts to the fear, how they behave in response to it. How does your child describe their fears, what are they so afraid of? And very importantly, how did this fear appear? Did it come on gradually and worsen over time or did just appear suddenly, "out of the blue" with no apparent reason, or was it a reaction to an event that they should have easily gotten over? All of this information assists the health care provider or mental health specialist to figure out just what is going on and to come up with a treatment plan to resolve the problems.

As a parent you should be directly and actively involved in both the diagnostic and treatment process. You are the person who knows your child the best and you need to feel comfortable with the therapist or other treatment provider. Just like all human beings, therapists have different personalities and might use different methods. If for some reason you do not feel comfortable with the therapist working with your child you may want to find another one who is a better fit for you and your child. After reading this book you may decide against therapy and tackle the job on your own using the information contained herein. Whatever works best for you and your family. You get to decide.

The following chapters list the various types of Anxiety Disorders experienced by young children that will help you understand and identify what's going on with the child. Your understanding can be very helpful in the treatment process and helps you know more about what to expect. Knowledge is empowering. When we know better we do better.

DIAGNOSES

Before we begin to talk about diagnoses I think it is important for me not to beat around the bush, but come right out and say that I do not like diagnoses. They put a label on the child. Sometimes there is a tendency to treat the label and not the child. A child is a child, not their disorder. However, as a mental health provider working in the medical community, you cannot get paid unless you have a diagnosis to put on the file along with it's number because that is the only thing insurance companies who pay the bills will recognize. Since they are a necessary evil let's talk about them.

There are a few Anxiety Disorders that occur or begin in childhood including, Generalized Anxiety Disorder, Panic Disorder and Separation Anxiety Disorder. Sometimes children may be diagnosed with other disorders such as Oppositional Defiant Disorder or Conduct Disorder. They all have both similar and different symptoms and causes. I try to be very careful with diagnoses because it is so easy to put a raspberry label on a jar of strawberry jam. They're both berries, both taste good, and both go great with peanut butter in sandwiches. Yet they're not quite the same. And it might not be jam at all. I approach diagnoses slowly and carefully.

Over my 20 some years of experience I have seen numerous cases where children came into treatment diagnosed with ADD/ADHD, Oppositional Defiant Disorder or Conduct Disorder only to find six months or so down the road that it was an Anxiety Disorder all along but the child's behavior got in the way of seeing it. Plus mental health professionals and doctors have to list a diagnosis, any diagnosis, as I mentioned previously in order to get paid. And it has to be done right away. This is often how mistakes are made. Just because a child has been labeled as raspberry jam we should all keep an open mind that they might be strawberry jam or not jam at all.

I have used a variety of resources to try and explain this process to all who may have an interest in how it all works. The initial information is written in lay terms (for everybody) and is easy to understand and offers more information to parents than a diagnostic manual used by professionals might. Particularly the tips on what symptoms to look for and what to do when you ask for help.

First I will list information gotten from the internet and then I will discuss the Diagnostic and Statistical Manual, 4th Edition TR (DSM IV) which is the book used by professionals to make a diagnostic decision.

GENERALIZED ANXIETY DISORDER

What is Generalized Anxiety Disorder?

A child with generalized anxiety disorder is generally fearful, but not related to any specific thing. Although they may develop fears of monsters in the closet or other irrational, imaginary fears, it is not in response to a single event or series of events.

How does it occur?

Generalized Anxiety Disorder develops many times in the child's own imagination or self talk. Self talk is what we say/hear inside our head, always in our own voice, such as I'm ugly, when, in fact this is not true. Adults do this all the time and we learned it in early childhood.

Children are expert listeners but lousy interpreters. Remember the phrase "little pitchers have big ears? Well, it's true. Unfortunately, children often overhear adult conversations and totally misconstrue what is being said. This can lead to an anxiety problem. The child believes something bad is going to happen, which is not true, but yet they *believe* it to be so. Children often assume responsibility, or blame, for bad things happening which increases the possibility of the development of an anxiety disorder. Just a simple disagreement between parents can become a really big deal because the child may make the assumption their parents are headed for divorce court.

Sometimes Anxiety Disorders have a genetic component. Anxious parents have anxious children. Children pick up on nonverbal cues easily, so no matter how hard we try to keep our fears a secret, our actions are often affecting our children. Temperament, which also has a genetic component, can be a contributor as well. Parents who are quiet and shy may have children who display similar behaviors. Sometimes, however, the opposite may be true. A quiet, calm parent may have an active, assertive child and this difference in temperament can be part of the problem and the parent's ability to cope. This is quite normal unless or until it becomes disruptive to the child and the family and then it's time to seek help from a professional who works with young children with emotional difficulties.

What are the symptoms?

Unlike other Anxiety Disorders, the onset of Generalized Anxiety Disorder comes on gradually over time. It may start with shyness and progress to being fearful of everything, even their own shadow.

- Your child becomes overly shy when they have been normally outgoing
- Your child overreacts when you leave them, even though you may just be in another room
- Your child develops fears of certain objects with no apparent reason or explanation, such as dogs or the dark.
- Your child develops nightmares and may refuse to sleep in their own room.
- Your child develops unexplained fears of normal daily routines such as using the bathroom as in the case of Keri and Meredith.
- Your child expresses fear of imaginary objects or beings.

How is it diagnosed?

Before you begin any kind of mental health treatment for your child you should have your child be seen by their pediatrician or family doctor to rule out any physical cause for the problem. Your doctor may be able to refer you to a therapist who specializes in working with young children.

Your child's health care provider or mental health therapist can tell you if your child suffers from this disorder. They use a variety of means to reach this conclusion. As a mental health therapist, I often asked parents, grandparents and pre-school teachers to complete a form called the Achenbach Child Behavior Checklist (CBCL). This is a well researched and fairly accurate instrument that assists in viewing the child's behaviors through the eyes of all the adults regularly involved in the child's life. The CBCL will show if your child is introverted or extroverted and what kinds of behaviors the child exhibits. It's a long questionnaire with a bazillion questions, but the questions are all designed to create a pretty accurate picture of the child and accuracy is the goal we all aim for.

Mental health therapists will also conduct an in depth interview with you and your child as well as using other types of questionnaires that assist in reaching an accurate diagnosis for your child. Each therapist has their own routine they follow to reach a diagnosis and it is most often accurate. They are well trained in this procedure and have multiple resources to assist them, such as the DSM IV.

How is it treated?

The goals of anxiety therapy are to increase the child's ability to self soothe and relax: to assess and augment positive coping strategies; to help implement coping strategies; and to recognize successes and build on them.

Different therapist use a variety of techniques to help your child including play therapy or cognitive-behavioral therapy, which is basically talking with your child and helping them develop the skills they need to learn to cope with their fears. They may also teach you new ways to change the behavior. In this book the use of magical allies is recommended as an integral part of the treatment plan.

After the completion of the intake process wherein I employ the use of the Achenbach Child Behavior Checklist, completed by both parents and sometimes other family members or teachers, to rule out other disorders, and a diagnosis of Anxiety Disorder is made. At this time I begin to introduce magical thinking therapy. Magical thinking can both create the problems and cure the problems. This is where play therapy can be an effective tool in relieving the child's fears. This method works particularly well with pre-school aged children.

PANIC DISORDER

What is panic disorder?

A child with panic disorder (PD) has sudden attacks of fear or severe anxiety that lasts for a short period of time, but reoccurs. The fearful attacks happen several times over weeks or months. They may last a few minutes or they may last for hours. All children feel fearful at times, however. The fear is usually brief, and goes away without causing major problems. Panic disorder is when the fearful times happen over and over, start suddenly without a clear cause, and are severe. PD interferes greatly in daily life at home, in school or even in the grocery store.

Panic attacks are not caused by fear of a single thing or event. That is called a phobia, like being scared of dogs or the dark. The attacks are also not caused by a traumatic event, like child abuse or being in a car accident. If caused by trauma, the child may have Post Traumatic Stress Disorder (PTSD).

How does it occur?

PD begins most often in the late teen years into adulthood. It does, however, sometimes start in early childhood. It begins with a few attacks that come and go. Often it never goes beyond this, but some children start having attacks often that increase in number and severity.

A stressful event, like parents divorcing or a move to a new place, may trigger the panic. But often PD begins with no identified stressful event. It is common for children to have periods of time with attacks and then go weeks or months with few or none. Then the attacks may return with a vengeance with frequent events that disrupt the life of the child and family and then, as with other disorders, it is time to seek help.

What are the symptoms?

Panic attacks, just like those in adults, tend to come on suddenly with no warning. Children may:

- Cry in fear
- Tremble or shake
- Be short of breath or feel like they are smothering
- Feel like they are choking or have trouble swallowing
- Feel their heart pounding
- Feel they are going to die or that they are going crazy
- Feel very helpless to stop or control the attacks
- Display an intense startle reflex
- Eat very little or become picky eaters
- Have trouble concentrating during an event or due to the fear an event will occur unexpectedly
- Have frequent headaches or stomach aches
- Have trouble falling or staying asleep or develop nightmares

Panic attacks often happen at certain times of the day, such as at bedtime, or with daily events, for example, going to school. When this is the case, the child often worries as these times approach. However, most often panic attacks occur without warning and can happen at anytime anywhere. This causes the child to feel helpless and out of control, unable to predict or prevent an attack. This results in a general increase of anxiety so the child will actually have a dual diagnosis of Anxiety Disorder as well as Panic Disorder.

How is it diagnosed?

Usually it is diagnosed due to the reports of the suddenness of onset and the physical symptoms reported above. Children almost always also present with the usual symptoms of Anxiety Disorder, but the sudden attacks accompanied by the physical symptoms are good indicators the child has this problem.

How is it treated?

PD is treated much the same as all anxiety disorders in children. However, there are some specific things that can be done when an attack occurs. A parent or caregiver can take the child aside and talk to them in a calm, quiet manner and encourage them to take deep, slow breaths (deep breathing), and to soothe the child as best they can as the child has lost the ability to self soothe during the attack. Sometimes holding the child and rocking them helps, but at other times will increase the feelings of being smothered. It is best to let the child be the guide as to what helps and what doesn't. Many times they have learned from experience what works for them. When in doubt follow your best instincts and use the normal soothing, calming techniques until the attack passes. Panic attacks occur without warning and can happen in public places that can be incredibly embarrassing to the child, so it is best to remove the child to a calmer, quieter and more private setting whenever possible.

Cognitive-Behavioral Therapy helps children learn what causes them to feel panic and how to control it. CBT teaches specific skills for managing the fear and the worrisome thoughts about whether an attack is coming. I employ the use of allies during this process. Having an ally, real or imaginary, makes he child feel less alone and more in control. They have a helper in their time of need. Having a helper can be incredibly empowering since a child suffering panic attacks feels so out of control. Having an ally helps restore a sense of control.

Family Therapy can often be helpful in cases of panic disorder. It is always helpful to have the family involved and it brings an added sense of support to the child. Also, an ally may be found within the family unit and that person can be of great assistance to the child. It is very important the child feel supported and reassured. What the child does not need is a brother or sister who laughs at them or makes fun of their distress. Family Therapy can be an effective intervention.

What can I do to help my child?

- Reassure your child that their feelings are understandable and that they are not "going crazy"
- Encourage your child to talk freely about their fears, but do not force it. Let them talk when they are ready

- Empower your child by letting them make simple decisions when appropriate. It gives them a sense of control.
- Repeatedly tell your child it is not their fault.
- Keep in touch with other family members, caregivers, teachers; anybody regularly involved with your child so you are able to track attacks and perhaps employ them as allies.
- Avoid criticizing your child for acting younger than their age. If they need a light on at night, turn on a light.
- Make sure your child gets enough sleep and exercise every day.
- Avoid letting your child have any kind of stimulants, such as caffeine in colas.
- Seek help when you feel you need it. If your family life is disrupted by the panic attacks then it might be wise to intervene with professional help.
- Some pediatricians, family doctors and psychiatrists may recommend the use of medication which can be helpful for the short term, but only if what you are already doing isn't working. Medication should be the last resort whenever possible. If you have faith and trust in your medical provider then, by all means, follow their recommendations.
- Take good care of yourself. If you are too tired or emotionally drained you will not be fully available to support your child.

SEPARATION ANXIETY DISORDER

What is it?

When you leave your child in the care of another person it can be stressful for both the child and the parent. For the child, the fear elated to the parent leaving his or her sight is called Separation Anxiety. This is a completely normal reaction, particularly in certain developmental stages of infancy. Normally, once the parent leaves, the child stops crying and moves on to another activity. Separation anxiety is most common between the ages of 6 months and 2 years of age. Beyond that, if the child's reaction is severe, they are not able to be soothed in a reasonable amount of time, or they continue to express fear that is not age appropriate whenever a parent is out of sight, and it is disrupting to the parent and family, then it is time to seek help.

How can I help?

There are many things a parent can do to help their child during times when they must be left with a caregiver or teacher.

- Do not talk about leaving beforehand.
- Plan ahead so you can separate quickly. Have everything you need in one bag so it can be dropped of quickly.
- When it's time for you to leave, do so as matter-of-factly and quickly as possible. Dragging out the drama only increases the child's sense of fear.
- Do not sneak away when your child is not looking. They may feel betrayed and abandoned.

- Practice separating several times for short durations so the child gets used to you returning.
- Reassure your child you will come back as soon as you can, such as after work. You can give them a time and they can watch a clock if they are at an age they can do so.
- When you pick your child up don't be overly emotional. It's okay to be glad to see them, but avoid crying and hugging too much. Such behavior feeds into the fear.
- Generally, if the parent is calm and matter-of-fact when they drop off their child, the child will respond in kind. If the parent remains calm and reassuring it helps the parting of ways.
- Although it is normal for a child to cry when a parent leaves, if the parent acts soothingly, but does not buy into the drama the separation goes much smoother.
- Deal with your own emotions. It is hard to leave your child in the care of another, particularly if you work. You need to come to terms with your own feelings of guilt so you reduce the chance you will over react when you pick up your child.
- Find a caregiver you trust. It makes it easier to leave your child with them.

How long does it last?

Separation Anxiety should begin to drop off after the age of 2. It should also decrease as your child becomes accustomed to being left. If your child knows their caregiver, or as they come to know them, the behavior should decrease or stop. However, I have experienced a 5 year old child who would literally scream non-stop for hours until he was exhausted whenever his mother left him, even when it was with his grandmother. No amount of soothing could slow this kid down and it was not improving over time. It was a disaster for both the parent and the child, not to mention the poor caregiver who had to endure the screaming day after day. This was definitely a case for professional intervention.

How is it treated?

Generally speaking Family Therapy seems to work the best. The child's fear of separation is often in direct correlation with their parent's actions. In the case described above with the 5 year old boy, it was discovered that the mother treated this boy more like an infant than a 5 year old. He still rode in a stroller even though he was fully capable of walking. She also fed him even though he was fully capable of eating on his own and did so in settings when his mother was not there. It seemed that her babying him made him feel overly dependent on her. Once the mother was empowered to treat the boy more age appropriately, the child was empowered and felt more in control and eventually the stressful departures dropped off.

It is quite normal for young children to cry when a parent leaves them. It is critical to discuss this with the caregiver who can give information about how long the crying lasts once the parent leaves. Knowing the crying stops the minute the parent walks out the door makes it easier for the parent to leave them the next time. It is also critical that you know and trust the caregiver. There are times when a child's fear has a real basis as in the cases of abusive caretakers. I think it is important to recognize the existence of this problem and to not automatically rule it out particularly if the fear reaction is severe and ongoing with little or no improvement over time even with professional intervention.

THE DSM IV

The DSM IV is the Diagnostic and Statistical Manual of Mental Disorders, Fourth Edition, Text Review; 2000, American Psychiatric Association. It is the book used by mental health professionals to determine a diagnosis for their clients. The following is a direct quote from this manual.

*Note: with the exception of Separation Anxiety Disorder Specify if: Early Onset: if it occurs before the age of 6 years.

Anxiety Disorders:

- Panic Attack
- Agoraphobia
- Specific Phobia characterized by clinically significant anxiety provoked by exposure to a specific feared object or situation, often leading to avoidance behavior.
- Social Phobia is characterized by clinically significant anxiety provoked by exposure to certain types of social or performance situations, often leading to avoidance behavior.

Generalized Anxiety Disorder: is characterized by at least 6 months of persistent and excessive anxiety and worry. **Overanxious Disorder of Childhood:** In children and adolescents with Generalized Anxiety Disorder, the anxieties and worries often concern the quality of their performance or competence at school. They may worry about catastrophic events such as earthquakes or nuclear war. Children with the Disorders may be overly conforming, perfectionist, and unsure of themselves. One half of adults presenting with this Disorder report onset in childhood.

Diagnostic Criteria for 300.02 Generalized Anxiety Disorder:

A. Excessive anxiety and worry (apprehensive expectation), occurring more days than not for at least 6 months, about a number of events or activities.

B. The person finds it difficult to control the worry

C. The anxieties and worry are associated with 3 (or more) of the following six symptoms with at least some symptoms present for more days than not for the past 6 months. **Note: Only one item is required in children** (my bold type).

- 1. restlessness or feeling keyed up or on edge
- 2. being easily fatigued
- 3. difficulty concentrating or mind going blank
- 4. irritability
- 5. muscle tension
- 6. sleep disturbance (difficulty falling or staying asleep, or restless unsatisfying sleep). Nightmares.

The focus of anxiety is not related to symptoms of other types of Disorders.

Diagnostic Criteria for 309.21 Separation Anxiety Disorder

Diagnostic features: excessive anxiety concerning separation from home or from those to whom the person is attached (criterion A). This anxiety is beyond that which is expected for the individual's developmental level. The disturbance must last for a period of at least 4 weeks (criterion B), begin before 18 years of age (criterion C) and cause clinically significant distress or impairment in social, academic, or other important areas of functioning.

Tend to come from families that are close knit. When separated from home or major attachment figures, they may recurrently exhibit social withdrawal, apathy, sadness or difficulty concentrating on work or play. Depending on their age, individuals may have fears of animals, monsters, the dark, muggers, burglars, kidnappers, car accidents, plane travel, and other situations that are perceived as presenting danger to the integrity of the family or themselves. Concerns about death or dying are common. School refusal may lead to academic difficulties and social avoidance. Children may complain that no one loves them or cares about them and that they wish they were dead. When extremely upset at the prospect of separation they may show anger, or occasionally hit out at someone who is forcing separation . . . children with this Disorder are often described as demanding, intrusive, and in need of constant attention. The child's excessive demands often become a source of parental frustration, leading to resentment and conflict in the family. Sometimes children with the Disorder are described as unusually conscientious, compliant, and eager to please. The children may have somatic complaints that result in physical examinations and medical procedures.

It is important to differentiate Separation Anxiety Disorder from the high value some cultures place on strong interdependence among family members.

Separation Anxiety Disorder is not uncommon; prevalence estimates average about 4% in children and young adolescents. Separation Anxiety Disorder decreases in prevalence from childhood through adolescence.

Separation Anxiety Disorder may develop after some life stress (e.g. the death of a relative or pet, an illness of the child or a relative, a change of schools, a move to a new neighborhood or immigration). Onset may be as early as pre-school age and may occur at any age prior to 18 years.

It is relatively more frequent in children of mothers with Panic Disorder.

Diagnostic Criteria:

A. Developmentally inappropriate and excessive anxiety concerning separation from home or those to whom the individual is attached, as evidenced by three (or more) of the following:
- 1. Recurrent excessive distress when separation from home or major attachment figures occurs or is anticipated
- 2. Persistent and excessive worry about losing a major attachment figure
- 3. Persistent and excessive worry that an untoward event will lead to separation from a major attachment figure (e.g. getting lost or being kidnapped)

- 4. Persistent reluctance or refusal to go to school or elsewhere because of fear of separation
- 5. Persistently and excessively fearful or reluctant to be alone or without major attachment figures at home or without significant adults in other settings
- 6. Persistent reluctance or refusal to go to sleep without being near a major attachment figure or to sleep way from home
- 7. Repeated nightmares involving themes of separation
- 8. Repeated complaints of physical symptoms (such as headaches, stomachaches, nausea, or vomiting) when separation from major attachment figures occurs or is anticipated

B. The duration of the disturbance is at least 4 weeks.
C. Onset is before age 18 years
D. The disturbance causes clinically significant distress or impairment in social, academic, (occupational), or other important areas of function
E. The disturbance does not occur exclusively during the course of a Pervasive Developmental Disorder, Schizophrenia, or other Psychotic Disorder and, in adolescents and adults, is not better accounted for by Panic Disorder and Agoraphobia"

Other Disorders mentioned but no criteria is listed for children such as the following:

Agoraphobia is the fear of leaving one's home, being outside or in open areas. Your child may cry and be overly clingy whenever you leave the house or perhaps go to the mall with its wide open spaces. It is often confused with Separation Anxiety Disorder.

Panic Attacks are sudden onset and severe anxiety that occurs "out of the blue" with no apparent reason. It is often accompanied by sweating, feelings of heart palpitations or rapid heart beat, or feeling as if one might faint. Children react differently to this disorder than adults but it is the sudden onset and reoccurrence that leads one to believe this may be the problem.

Specific Phobias are fears and severe anxiety associated with a certain object. "It is characterized by clinically significant anxiety provoked by exposure to a specific feared object or situation, often leading to avoidance behavior", such as the fear of dogs.

Social Phobia "is characterized by clinically significant anxiety provoked by exposure to certain types of social or performance situations, often leading to avoidance behavior" such as a school play, concert, or a musical or dance recital.

WHAT ARE ALLIES?

Okay, so now you pretty much understand all you need to know about Anxiety Disorders in children and it has been decided that your child may have such a Disorder. Where do we go from here? As you have read there are a number of things you can do to try and help your child, but I have a new and inventive method of treating Anxiety Disorders in children using what I refer to as allies. I have used this method on many occasions, with many clients and children from the ages of 3 to 12 with significant success. I have found this method to be easier on the child and the family and the results come sooner than with other methods of dealing with such problems. So let's talk about allies.

According to Webster's Collegiate Dictionary, Tenth Edition; an ally is "one that is associated with another as a helper". The American Heritage Dictionary defines an ally as "one united or connected in a formal or close relationship or bond" and an alliance is defined as "a union, relationship or connection by kinship, marriage or common interest". In anxiety disorders the common bond is fear and worry.

For the purposes of this book, allies can be parents, friends, relatives or animals, all real or imagined. An ally can literally be anything or anybody the child is able to place their trust in and who can help them tackle their fears.

Children suffering from an Anxiety Disorder have lost their sense of control. They have lost their sense of safety. And they have lost their creativity. Whatever is causing their fears is much bigger than they are in every way and they need a helper to assist them in getting back all they have lost. They have lost their self—esteem and no longer see themselves as the capable kids we all know they are. It damages their self—esteem.

In their book, *Self Esteem*, Matthew McKay and Patrick Fanning state "Studies of young children show clearly that parents style of child rearing during the first 3-4 years determines the amount of self-esteem that child starts with. Self-esteem is essential for psychological survival. It is an emotional *sine qua non*. One of the main factors differentiating humans from other animals is the awareness of self: the ability to form an identity and then attach a value to it. The problem with self-esteem is the human capacity for judgement (self-criticism)". Anxiety decreases a child's natural abilities to do what they have always done before, but no longer work; such as self-soothing. They lose faith in themselves. They no longer value themselves as they may have in the past. In treating anxious children it is imperative to find ways to empower the child and help them to return to their belief in their own competence and give them back their self-esteem.

According to Judith McKay, R.N., "The child with good self-esteem has the best chance of being a happy and successful adult. Self-esteem is the armor that protects kids from the dragons of life: drugs, alcohol, unhealthy relationships and delinquency. The fears, limits and feelings of helplessness adults struggle with today have existed from the earliest years". This reinforces my position that it is critical to treat a child's anxiety problems early on before it has a chance to permanently damage the child's psyche and sense of self-esteem. All children express fears and anxiety at some point in their lives, but when it lasts longer than what is normally expected and disrupts the family life, it is time to take action and seek some kind of help. Fortunately there is an increased awareness of these kinds of problems and a plethora of information is available plus there is a decrease in the stigma of seeking help from a mental health professional, all of which bode well for the child.

Children with anxiety disorders have lost their ability to self soothe. Whatever they have used in the past to make themselves feel better is just not working anymore. Their favorite blanket or toy has lost their gift of comfort. No matter how many hugs or comforting words are offered in an attempt to allay their fear it is not getting the job done.

Sometimes an ally can be as simple as leaving a light on or having a nightlight when a child is afraid of the dark. The light simply makes the dark go away. Or, as in least two of my example stories, the ally is a simple, humble broom. It doesn't have to be a big deal. What is important is the child *believes*.

THE MIGHTY THUMB

I remember a time when my younger brother, who was about 5 at the time, developed a fear of some older, bigger boys at school who were bullying him and he was afraid to go to school and felt powerless to deal with them. A friend of my parents told him if he blew on his thumb really hard it would pump up his bicep muscles and then he would become stronger and then could beat his fear of these bullies who were causing him so much fright. So my brother blew and blew on his thumb until his face got beet red. Then he would make a muscle to check and see if it was working. And, of course, it was. Everyone could see it. Even his evil big sister got in on the act, carefully checking out the growing muscle. Oh yes, it was much bigger! It worked wonderfully because my brother *believed* it was. His belief in his newly found muscles enabled him to stand up to the bullies who never bothered him again. However, it is rarely quite so simple.

MORE ON ALLIES

Most often you have to get quite creative to find an ally that works for the child. One the child believes in and can place their trust in.

In her book *Allies In Healing,* Laura Davis, although it deals primarily with sexual abuse survivors the needs are similar, Davis describes the best characteristics of an adult ally as having the following characteristics:

- Compassion
- Flexibility
- Resourcefulness
- Patience
- Sense of humor
- Knowledge of their own needs and limits

When dealing with an anxious child things can often become topsy-turvy and the person serving as an ally to that child must be able to roll with the changes, adjust their expectations and meet their own neglected needs. The anxious child may be quite needy and thrives on extra attention. The adult ally must be comfortable with setting limits for the child and to take care of themselves or they can be easily drained physically and emotionally. Setting limits and boundaries for the child also can be comforting to the child by giving them structure plus they know what to expect will happen and therefore increases their sense of trust. All children need rules and limits to build their lives around. They give children a sense of belonging and safety, but anxious children, because they have lost their ability to self soothe need them even more.

Children are the experts in their lives. They know themselves the best but they do not always have the means of expressing themselves. Their vocabulary is often limited. Even though they may not be able to articulate their fears they may be able to draw them. Or with some assistance they can become able to verbalize what is causing them so much discomfort by helping them find the right words. Sometimes simply brainstorming with the child can lead to a mutual understanding of the problem the child is facing. Accurately seeing children builds self-esteem in 4 ways. 1st is the ability to recognize their unique abilities and talents. 2nd is the ability to understand their behavior in the context of who they are. 3rd, seeing children accurately allows focus on only changing the target behaviors that are harmful to them, isolates them socially or is disruptive to the family. It takes some time and effort to accurately see the child as who they really are, not just that they have an Anxiety Disorder.

In working with children all these many years I have come to rely on two wonderful women who have co-authored several books that have been most helpful to me, Adele Faber and Elaine Mazlich. Together they have written: *How to Talk so Children will Listen and Listen so Children will Talk; Liberated Parents/Liberated Children;* and *Without Spanking or Spoiling.* I have kept these 3 books in my library even though I am now retired. I have grandchildren so I sometimes need to be reminded of what I already know but sometimes forget. I have recommended these books to virtually all of the parents who were my clients, friends or family. These 3 books are incredibly helpful in developing the ability to accurately see the child as they are. I have also recommended *"How To Talk . . .* to cohorts and anyone who works with young children in any capacity from attorneys, to teachers or caregivers and especially parents. They are wonderful books full of humor and wisdom and I highly recommend them to anyone reading this book.

Whatever it is that causes the child to be anxious and fearful does not occur in a vacuum. It is, therefore, critical to look closely at the family dynamics. Particularly when no imaginary ally can be found or is not effective and you must search for a real live person to fill the position.

Some cultures have allies already built into their belief system. For example, Native Americans have Totems, Fetishes and Dream Catchers.

Totems are animal spirits that have special powers and serve as spirit guides and protectors. Some Native American families or organizations place totem poles near a home or building, carved from wood, usually a cedar tree with several spirit animals represented in the carving and are believed to protect the home or business from harm.

Fetishes are small objects, usually carved from stone that may have special meaning or power, that resemble or represent animal spirit protectors or guides. Fetishes are believed to have some characteristic of the animal spirit it is carved to represent. For instance the otter is playful and happy. Coyotes are tricksters. Mother Bear is protective. Fetishes are given to a person who has a particular need that the fetish can satisfy or as a representation of a facet of a person's personality. Fetishes are carried in either pockets or pouches and can be held or rubbed in one's hand(s) when overcome by fear or worry. Much like a worry stone.

Jane Kirkpatrick wonderfully describes Dream Catchers in her book *A Sweetness To The Soul* about early life in the Oregon Territory. She describes it as; "Round and wrapped in rawhide with a feather hanging from the leather, its center is crisscrossed like a spider with sinew. A bead or stone symbolizing the mythical goodness of the spider forms the center; the feather represents the eagle, the only bird believed to fly between the dream world and our own. Hung over a child's bed while they sleep, the spider web catches the child's bad dreams to be burned by the sun in the morning; the good dreams know their way through and wait-to be chased by the child into the future". As a foster parent living near a large Reservation and being acquainted with the use of Dream Catchers, I put one in the bedroom window of a child who suffered from severe anxiety, particularly that someone would come in the window and "get" him. I read and told him stories about the Dream Catcher and then hung it in the window. The nightmares stopped and the anxiety began to ebb away. I have a small Dream Catcher that hangs on our family's antique bassinette to protect our newest family member. To this day I have a Dream Catcher hanging in at least one room of my house.

Native American Tribes in Alaska have a creature that lives in the spirit world who is said to snatch up naughty children. I have an artistic representation of this creature hanging on the wall in my guest room. I have told the story to my grandchildren, who don't buy it for a minute once they are past three, but before then they are believers and tend to avoid going near the painting. It does look sort of fierce. Although this spirit creature is meant to frighten children into being good it points to the strength of the belief system that these animal spirits are a part of and that has been passed on from generation to generation for hundreds of years.

Working with and being friends with Native Americans from the Confederated Colville Tribes I learned about the concept of "Aunties". Aunties are usually older women who may or may not be related by blood, but are viewed as helpers. Children are taught from birth to trust and have faith in their Aunties. Children may have only one Auntie, but usually there are several. Aunties would be an excellent resource for finding an effective ally for a frightened child.

Other cultures have their own characters or critters that possess magical powers. The Irish have their Leprechauns and Faeries.

Most oriental cultures have an expanded family structure from what we know here in the Western world. Elderly people are treated with honor and respect for their wisdom. They do not send the elderly family members to an assisted living facility or nursing home, but rather they keep them at home. The whole family continues to live together as a unit with multiple generations. Children grow up hearing the stories told by their elders and are taught to believe in their wisdom. Such practice is like an open pathway to an ally. When you have someone who lives with you who is held in such high esteem it would seem natural a child might turn to their grandparents or great grandparents in their time of need.

Other cultures also maintain an expanded family unit. In some countries in the Middle East the entire family lives in a compound with each having their own house that revolves around a main house that usually belongs to the family elders. When there is a marriage a new house is added. The family gathers in the central home for family activities and meals. Having so many relatives close by also would naturally increase the options of successfully finding an ally within the child's family.

Once again I stress treating the "whole" child. Rather than focusing totally on the child and their anxiety it is important to know about their life and the world they exist in. Knowing more about the family, who is in it and what are their beliefs? Where does the child fit in? Are they an oldest child, a middle child, a youngest child or an only child? Are the parents in tact or separated, is there custodial problems, are both parents involved in the child's life and do their parenting styles differ? All of this information helps give you an *accurate* picture of the child.

Some families might be against the use of imaginary allies, particularly one's you help the child create, because they may have religious beliefs against such a practice. Best to check beforehand.

In the current Fall Preview 2010 of the Signals Catalogue on page 24 they offer for purchase "Scaremenot Plush Monsters". In this ad the toys are described as "Stop the bedtime scaries with cuddly, funny 'security monsters'. Winner of several prestigious awards (from Dr. Toy and the National Parenting Center, among others) these creatures are huggable confidantes and nightmare companions. Each is about 14"-19" high, with a long tail (with Velcro strip) to hang from a door handle, closet rod, or tuck between boxspring and mattress (so the monster can peer under the bed). Specify pink Defender Dave, blue Protector Patty, green Guardian Gus, or Orange Watchdog Wally". They sell for a nominal fee of $24.95 plus shipping and handling. A mere pittance if they work for a child. It seems everybody is getting into the use of allies these days. I am both surprised and pleased these toys are described as *confidantes and companions.* That is precisely what allies do for anxious children. Whoever developed these toys has a good understanding of children's fears and how to help the child cope with them.

An ally can also be an animal, perhaps a family pet. I distinctly remember when I was a young child I used to share my worries, fears and all my varied feelings with a cat or a dog. We always had at least one pet as I was growing up. When I was about 10 my parents bought me a horse. I have many memories of pouring out my heart with my arms around his neck or lying on his back. To this day the smell of horses brings back many fond memories of my best friend. Living in a remote area of northeastern Oregon it was very common to see little girls on horseback and I often wondered how many tears and fears were being shared from child to horse.

My younger brother was very attached to our dog, "Tuffy", who was our faithful pet throughout our childhood years clear up through high school. I am sure Tuffy listened to my brothers secrets and protected him night and day.

My second son was very attached to his cat, "Charles", who used to sleep wrapped around Mike's head making sure all his dreams were sweet ones. Mike also had his "blankie", sucked his thumb, twirled his hair and had a stuffed toy "Casper the friendly ghost stuffed toy, all of which soothed him and gave him comfort. However, when Casper was lost or stolen, Mike was unable to sleep and his appetite greatly decreased and nothing could console him. He ultimately got over it but it was a hard time for both him and me.

It is not important who or what becomes the ally. What is important is that the child believes *as if* it were true. By allowing the child to describe their fear it is an easy switch to allow them to describe their ally in the case of an imaginary friend. Using words that are descriptive such as colors, numbers, size, furry or bald, and so forth, you can establish a rapport with the child about the source(s) of their fear.

Once you have established a clear understanding of their fears you can begin to work on identifying an ally to challenge the cause of the anxiety. No matter whether the chosen ally is real or imaginary they all hold some special *sense of magic or power* in the child's mind. It is this belief that gives the ally the ability to chase away fears and worries that young children often have, no matter the cause.

CHARACTERISTICS OF A GOOD ALLY

Any good ally posses the following general characteristics:

- Patience and lots of it
- A good listener
- Is empathetic/sympathetic
- Is readily available
- Is friendly
- Is trustful, can keep secrets
- Has some kind of power, real or magical that makes them stronger than the cause of the anxiety. These special powers may already exist as in the case of Susan and her father, or be created as in the case of Mrs. Mouse.
- Is resourceful
- Is always on the child's side. They do not correct the child's grammar or try to convince them otherwise. They simply accept what the child gives them to work with.

With very young children, particularly pre-schoolers, the very best allies have some kind of special, or magical, powers either real or imagined.

In the case of Mrs. Mouse I used the natural abilities mice really do have such as good eyesight, can see in the dark, have a good sense of smell and are small enough to fit in the tiniest spaces. Good qualities for a spy don't you think? In a case where Grandpa is the chosen ally you can do the same thing, using their natural abilities and qualities. Grandpa doesn't wear glasses so he must have good eyes. He is very tall and much bigger than monsters who are small enough to fit in a closet. Grandpa has big muscles so he is very strong. That kind of thinking. Don't be afraid to get creative, but do be honest. In both the case of Mrs. Mouse and the Wayward Lion the mothers are armed with their trusty, dusty brooms they use to shoo the fearful creatures away.

USING ALLIES THERAPEUTICALLY

Tips For Therapists and Parents

Initially I use generally accepted play therapy techniques such as drawing, playing games or free play to get to know more about the child and to establish a comfortable and trusting relationship.

Once a solid relationship is formed I begin to question the child's use of magical thinking. Do they have any imaginary friends? How do they describe their fears? Are magical creatures involved somehow? If not can magical thinking be employed to counteract the child's described fear? Can an imaginary ally be created? Is an imaginary ally needed or is a real one available?

Imaginary allies, created by the child their self can be an incredibly powerful treatment tool. First of all, the solution comes from the child, which can, if and of itself, be incredibly encouraging. The success of identifying or creating such an ally can give the child an added sense of control which is helpful because their anxiety makes them feel so helpless.

Once an imaginary or real ally is identified or created, the relationship between the child and their ally should be strengthened. Giving this ally additional or stronger powers enables the child to then employ their ally to work against the irrational or imagined fear, particularly if imaginary creatures are involved somehow with the fear/anxiety. I cannot stress often enough that it is the child's *belief* that makes using an ally such a useful tool therapeutically.

HEROES AND VILLAINS

Who or what are figures young children see as either a hero (ally) or a villain (enemy). They are much too young to identify with the most popular heroes like Superman, Spiderman, or Batman. Although they are usually aware of these characters and the fact they have super powers. Some cartoon characters such as Ben 10 are cartoon children who possess superpowers.

Animated movies like The Incredibles, which is a film that features an entire family, both parents and children, who all possess certain super powers. Even the baby, Jack-Jack, has the power to transform himself into various creatures, like a shape shifter, and challenges his babysitter. Quite often children's favorite movies are the ones in which the children have the powers to save the world or solve the problems. One of the most popular children's cartoons, Inspector Gadget, gained its popularity for just such a reason. It was always the little girl and her dog that saved the day while the inept and bumbling adult detective laughingly entertained with his inabilities. Children love to see the children in stories become the heroes.

In other popular children's movies like Finding Nemo, Bambi, Cars and even Shreck, the heroes of the story overcome their problems or solve a mystery via the use of their friends (allies). Nemo has his friend, Dory, a forgetful but friendly regal blue tang fish and the rag tag but loyal tank fish on his side who help Nemo find his father. Bambi has Thumper, the friendly bunny who teaches Bambi about life and introduces him to all his forest friends who all help Bambi overcome the loss of his mother and become the King of the forest. In the animated movie Cars, the cocky race car, Lightning McQueen loses his way and ends up depending on a motley crew of forgotten and abandoned cars who befriend him and get him back on the track. The Ogre Shreck, in the land of far, far away, finds himself with the help of his friends, Donkey, Puss in Boots and Fiona. Even

Merlin, the magical misguided wizard and awkward Prince Arthur help Shreck along the way to finding his true self in the four part series of Pixar's animated feature films.

Cinderella has the mice and the birds that befriend her not only against the wicked stepmother and stepsisters, but against the evil cat too. And best of all in this story is the Fairy Godmother, the kindly wizardess with the magic wand that has the superpowers to create all kinds of magic to save Cinderella.

In the Wizard of Oz, the timeless tale of Dorothy and the tornado, she has Toto, the cute and fuzzy dog. Then comes the Cowardly Lion, who, under normal circumstances, would be fierce, but is afraid of his own shadow, the Scarecrow who has no brain and the Tin Man who wants badly to have a heart, who form an alliance to help one another. Even the all powerful Wizard turns out to be just a kind, grandfatherly sort of man. And the two most powerful characters of all; Glenda the good witch with her magic wand and the wonderful Ruby Slippers whose powers get Dorothy back to Kansas and Auntie Em.

Most pre-schoolers have seen one or more of these movies or are familiar with the stories, such as Bambi and easily recognize how the gentle creatures take on magical sorts of powers and befriend the main character of the story to a positive outcome. Therefore, it is not a huge stretch to use a sort of guided imagery with young children to help them create their own Thumper, Toto or Dory when a human ally either can't be found or does not work for some reason.

Although pre-school children are developmentally unable to truly understand and identify with the super heroes of older children, they can quickly recognize friends as allies. In each of the films and cartoon characters, the heroes all have some facet of their personality that gives them some extra power or skill that enables them to rise above and save the day. They hear about heroes and super powers from the media; older siblings, cousins or friends; or perhaps just by osmosis. Young children always have their information antennae actively searching out and receiving new and exciting information. They don't miss much.

They are able to assimilate this information and transcend it into their own little world of magic and pretend.

Using their own descriptive words young children describe friends and heroes (allies) normally as creatures who are warm and fuzzy. Soft to the touch. Often furry. Kind and caring. Friendly. Happy. Funny. Small. Much like Thumper, Cinderella's mice and birds, or Dory, Nemo's forgetful but faithful friend. They are nice not mean.

By contrast, they describe their nemeses as having big, sharp teeth, big shiny eyes, and often scales. They are loud and noisy. Mean. Angry. Big. Scary. Scruffy. They don't comb their hair or brush their teeth. But, like the once blustery and frightening Wizard of Oz they can be brought to bear with the use of the friendly allies with magical powers.

So how do we help youngsters develop these, small, warm fuzzy characters into beings powerful enough to defend against and defeat the bigger, meaner and louder villains? Magic, of course. Give them some character or magical power that transforms them into the sort of hero who can join with the child to solve the dilemma at hand. It doesn't have to be something huge, like in Ben 10 or The Incredibles. Remember Thumper was just a wise and faithful friend who was always there to help Bambi even through the worst of times. And Cinderella's mice and birds were small and powerless until they joined together to form an alliance.

In the case of a real live ally the child may think of the person, toy or animal as also having some special power. Remember the childhood argument of "my Dad can beat up your Dad"? Your Dad may have been the smallest, quietest, most unassuming person, but to a small child their Dad could move mountains. And we all know Moms have "eyes in the back of their heads" and have super powerful hearing. No matter what it is the child sees or feels that makes a person, pet or toy a good ally it is their *belief*. It may make so sense whatsoever to anyone else, but if it works for the child put it to good use.

THE WAYWARD LION

My first introduction to how magical thinking can be a useful tool in therapeutic work did not come from any doctor, therapist or professor, or even a book. It came from a good friend who just happened to be a great Mom.

Her eldest daughter "discovered" there was a lion living under the sofa. She would run and jump up on the sofa so the lion couldn't get her. She would not let her legs dangle for fear the lion would get her feet. She kept her legs tucked tight up under her body. To her this lion was as real as the air we breathe and no amount of reasoning or coaxing would dissuade her from her belief and her fear.

If her younger brother would try and pull her feet off the sofa, she would scream and cry in fear. To her, there was, in fact, a very large and dangerous lion living under the sofa. No amount of teasing from her little brother made her feel one bit better. It only made her angry.

She could describe the lion in great detail. It was a boy lion and he was very large. It did not matter to her at all that there was not enough room under the sofa for such a creature. He was there all right. He was brown and kind of scruffy. His hair was messy because he didn't have a brush to brush his hair with. She asked her brother to put a brush under the sofa so the lion could brush his hair, which according to her made him look so much better. But, even with his new hairdo, he was still very dangerous.

This went on for a number of weeks, gradually getting worse. It all came to a head when she decided it was too dangerous to even go into the room where the sofa was. The lion could come out from under the sofa and eat her alive. The lion was gaining power and her fears were getting worse and worse. She began to have nightmares about the lion coming out from under the sofa at night and roaming freely about the house. The lion was becoming increasingly more dangerous and gaining more power over this little girl's life.

The Mom was at her wits end. She had tried everything she could think of to reassure her daughter there was no lion under the sofa. "See, look, there's not enough room under the sofa for a big lion to live". No response. The little girl was convinced. "Lions don't live here, they only live in Africa and zoos". No response. The girl was unmoved. No amount of logic or rationalizing had any impact on changing this child's opinion.

Finally, in an act of pure desperation, the mother went and got her broom and announced loudly, "Okay Mr. Lion, it's time for you to go. My daughter is afraid of you and I don't like it one bit. So out you go!!" She began swishing the broom under the sofa all the while shouting; "shoo you lion, shoo, get out of here". As the battle continued the Mom began swishing and waving the broom about the living room, all the while shouting, "shoo, shoo, out, you get out. Go away"!

The mother chased the imaginary lion out from under the sofa, out of the living room, into the kitchen. Next she pretended the lion tried to hide behind the kitchen stove. Mom continued brandishing her broom dramatically about the kitchen and finally shooed the lion out the back door and said, "And don't you ever come back here again".

The two young children watched in awe as their mother waged this battle of epic proportions with the imaginary lion. She showed no fear of the once scruffy creature. Out the door he went never to return.

After witnessing this scene, the girl seemed to be satisfied the lion was indeed gone and began to get up and down from the sofa as she had always done before the lion's arrival. She would let her legs and feet dangle over the edge of the sofa once again and all signs of her fears and anxieties seemed to disappear as if by magic. She also stopped having nightmares. The lion had been defeated in battle. The Mom was victorious. Her mother became her ally against the lion and armed with a simple broom defeated the fierce lion soundly. This was a prime example of the use of a family member as an ally.

After the lion's defeat, Mom prepared some special treats the children particularly enjoyed and the three, Mom, daughter and brother, had a party to celebrate the lion's demise.

By giving recognition to her daughter's imagination and reacting to the situation as if it were real she was able to resolve the situation when no amount of reasoning, rationalizing, teasing nor any other form of communicating could reach her daughter and do away with her fears. Only by accepting her daughter's imagination as a reality was she able to intervene on her daughter's behalf. This Mom used her daughter's own magical thinking to resolve the issues at hand. It truly was as if by magic.

BEING CREATIVE

So far we have seen at least 2 cases of very creative problem solving used to alleviate a child's anxiety, the thumb used against bullies and the broom against the wayward lion. Both are pretty creative don't you think?

The level of creativity used to treat children's anxiety disorders is dependent, in part, on their age and developmental abilities,(i.e. speech). In the case of Meredith and the downstairs bathroom, Keri found that a creative solution-and a lot of patience helped. We used Meredith's own love of art. She loved drawing, painting and coloring. Using a child's own likes and skills can be used as a sort of ally to overcome fears. It is a very simplified form of art therapy.

During the course of treatment with Meredith she displayed the ability and desire to draw and paint. So during her sessions art supplies were made available should she choose to use them. Initially, the drawings were not connected to the bathroom problem. With some gradual, gentle prodding she was guided to draw her fears on her paper and add her own words to solve the dilemma. It took several tries to get them just right. When she was satisfied with her work and had convinced herself she had solved her fears, the pictures were then posted on the respective bathrooms. Meredith then began using the downstairs bathroom, tentatively at first, keeping the door open and the light on and gradually working up to using it on her own with the door shut. Creating her own solution empowered Meredith when no amount of coaxing or prodding from her mother had any impact. What she chose to include in her artwork addressed her troubles in a way that satisfied her need for help. Although it made little or no sense to anyone else the pictures met her needs and gave he the feelings of security she needed to carry on.

I have consistently found that when children are allowed to become part of the solution they progress much faster toward problem resolution.

Rather than developing a creature ally, or using a family member, Meredith's artistic ability was used to create, from her own imagination, drawings that became a sort of ally because she created in them some sort of protective power. Drawings may seem to be a silly form of ally, but Meredith believed in them, they worked for her, and that is all that really mattered.

Sometimes the creativity comes from the child alone, (as in Meredith's case)at other times it comes from the parent (the case of the wayward lion), but most often and most successfully it comes in the form of cooperation (the case of Mrs. Mouse). In all cases the solution was found only when the fears were given recognition as reality, which is simply seeing the problem from the child's viewpoint. No matter how irrational their fears may seem, they are very real indeed to the child.

THE CASE OF MRS. MOUSE

A mother brought her 4 year old daughter in to my office for help. Her daughter sincerely believed there were monsters living in her closet. And they watched her as she slept and might come out of the closet at night. The problem had progressed over time to the point that the girl would no longer sleep in her own room and often requested to sleep with her Mom. The situation was clearly out of hand and both mother and daughter were exhausted from lack of sleep. No amount of reasoning or pleading could budge this little girl from her fears. So, in final desperation, Mom brought her in to see me because she heard from friends that I had some success in treating young children's anxieties.

I agreed to accept the child as a patient and we began hourly sessions once a week.

Initially I asked the girl to describe the monsters in great detail. How many of them were there? Were they boys or girls or both? What color were they? How big or small were they? The more detail I could get the better. It helped me to understand the depth of her imagination and how much power the imaginary monsters had over her.

There were 10 monsters. Some were very big, some were medium and some were small. One was purple and had very large, pointy teeth (sort of Barney gone awry). He was the largest of the bunch. Another was green, medium sized and had slimy scales that glowed in the dark. One was pink, because she was a girl monster, and she had silver, shiny, pointy teeth. Two were brown and hairy, one large and one small. They both growled and had red eyes that glowed in the dark. This went on until she had vividly described each and every one. This took several sessions to complete.

I then met with the mother to ask if she had seen any movies, read any books or otherwise might have seen and heard anything like the girl described to me. There was nothing she could think of that could have triggered her imagination of the creatures in her closet. I asked if there were any toys that could possibly appear like what she described in her bedroom closet. There were not. This was pure imagination.

When working with young children with imaginary fears and anxieties I always accept that whatever triggers their fear is real. I never try to reason them out of their beliefs. Instead, I try to enter their magical world as it is. To try to understand in as much detail as I can what their fears are and how they affect the child and the family. I also ask what the family has done to try and deal with the problems. As part of the course of treatment, I regularly administered the Achenbach Child Behavior Checklist. This instrument is well researched and accepted in the field. I used it to assist in teasing out, if possible, the separation of Attention Deficit Disorders and Anxiety Disorders in order to develop a correct diagnosis and treatment plan. Having done all of this I proceeded to develop a plan of intervention.

It came to light that this little girl had an imaginary friend, Mrs. Mouse, who lived under her bed. Mrs. Mouse was quite friendly and the girl trusted her implicitly.

We began discussing the possibility of Mrs. Mouse having some sort of special power(s) that might make her a viable ally against the monsters. First of all she had very good eyes and could easily see in the dark. Given this ability Mrs. Mouse could watch the monsters even at night to assure they didn't come out of the closet. Further, Mrs. Mouse had very good ears and could hear if the monsters tried to come out. Also, Mrs. Mouse was awake at night, as that's when mice are most active, so she would be awake to keep an eye on the monsters. But Mrs. Mouse was very small so how could she do battle to defeat the monsters? Super powers!

So we set about giving Mrs. Mouse some powers to use against the closet monsters. She had sharp teeth and could chew through rope and even wood as mice do. She could run very fast as mice do. She could get through the tiniest of places and hide easily as mice do. And she told the little girl every thing the monsters did. Mrs. Mouse was a snitch.

Mrs. Mouse was also a great thinker as mice are very smart creatures and can often outwit the best of mouse traps. Mrs. Mouse, being the wise and smart creature she was, decided it would be a good idea to invite Mom to join the alliance. So it happened and Mom became an ally too.

The little girl introduced Mom to Mrs. Mouse and Mom said "How do you do?" and "Glad to meet you". Mom began providing treats for Mrs. Mouse to make her stronger. A few bread crumbs, a piece of cookie or carrot that somehow always managed to disappear in the night.

With Mrs. Mouse on guard the girl was able to sleep in her own bed giving Mom a huge break and both slept through the night.

Then one day (at my suggestion) Mom told the girl that she and Mrs. Mouse had a meeting and decided it was time for the monsters to go. Mom told her Mrs. Mouse had suggested using the ever ready and all powerful broom as in the Wayward Lion. So Mom went and got the broom and swished it about the bedroom. She took all the toys and shoes out of the closet so the monsters couldn't hide and swept the closet out thoroughly all the while shouting "Shoo, shoo". Those are powerful words. She shooed the monsters, one and all, out of the bedroom, down the stairs, down the hallway and out the front door and off the porch. This Mom could have won an academy award for her performance that day.

At my suggestion Mother and daughter then sat down and had cookies and milk to celebrate the demise of the closet monsters. Case solved. The anxieties disappeared and peace was restored to the home. And Mrs. Mouse was invited to the girl's birthday party (had her own invitation) and was given some cake crumbs under the table as a treat.

For those of you who might be worried that creating such imaginary friends can somehow cause psychological damage or dependence, I have not had one case where this occurred to my knowledge. Several months after the case of Mrs. Mouse, I had the occasion to meet the mother and daughter at the grocery store. Apparently Mrs. Mouse was no longer needed and had moved on to help another little girl. As far as I know this little girl grew up just fine as did the girl with the problem with the lion who is now an adult with two boys of her own.

PATIENCE PAYS OFF

When you as a therapist first come into contact with the parent(s) and child, they are at their wits end and the parent-child relationship has been damaged and is at jeopardy. Once the child's fears have been identified from the child's point of view, no matter how irrational it may seem, and a treatment ally or goal has been identified, you can then invite the parent in as an additional ally. Once the parent is involved, encourage them to be creative in finding their own solution whenever possible. This helps to repair and maintain a positive parent-child relationship. Sometimes, however, the parent-child relationship has been so damaged it is necessary to seek other allies in the child's life; a grandparent, teacher, neighbor; any adult the child has a strong bond with and trusts.

During treatment sessions it became clear that Julia, the girl with the bicycle problems, viewed her father as her ally/hero. She truly believed her father could do anything. She assigned him with some additional super powers. It was decided it was time to give bike riding another try. Joe was a willing participant and, using his super powers, he was able to come up with a solution that worked for them. With Joe's patience the ride to the park was a success and Julia was rewarded for her hard work and effort. She gradually became confident enough in herself that she no longer needed her father's super powers and she had some of her own and was able to go on short bike rides alone.

After consulting with friends, family and with their therapist, Joe realized the solution to the bicycle issue was to leave his own bike at home for a while and keep his bike trips with Julia short. "We started by going around the block a few times. Because I knew that each intersection was going to require coaching and perhaps walking alongside Julia until she felt confident, it was easier for me to just jog alongside her with her on her bike. We did this for over a month. But once she saw that she could handle herself just fine, she was willing to try a ride to the park-and I took my bike this time. She's still extra careful at intersections, but I hope that will always be the case". The fact that, aside from having super powers, Joe was willing to stick with it for the long haul made a huge difference in the outcome of this case. His patience to work with Julia over the course of a month made all the difference in the successful outcome.

Parents that are emotionally close to their children provide them with a secure base that allows the child to feel strong and then take on new challenges. Play with them, laugh with them, delight in them. Reading to them where they can be physically close, relaxed and having fun is powerful too.

Often times when families first come into your office seeking help and advice they may have forgotten how to play with their child because they are too busy "putting out fires". Having one child, the identified patient, with out of control anxieties can disrupt the entire family. Helping parents get back on track by suggesting certain activities, like reading and playing in the park go a long way to repair the parent-child bond. In Joe's case, that he was able to come up with an activity directly related to the problem in a way that succeeded is not always the norm. Some parents need a little guidance and not all of them have super powers. Yet.

Children internalize their self image from what they read about themselves in their parents' faces. A child struggling with anxieties is helped when they know that they are safe, they are loved and they are capable of overcoming any obstacles that they may face. While all of this sounds wonderful, it is sometimes not an easy task to accomplish. It is true that children can read "between the lines" and are not easily fooled. Verbal communication is relatively new to them and they retain their ability to recognize nonverbal signals. It is imperative to involve the parents as you are able over the course of treatment to enable them to become active allies in their child's recovery process by helping them to be aware of specific things they can do and to increase their awareness of their own feelings and fears so they do not interfere with forming an alliance with their child, such as showing fear in their eyes. A young child will pick up on their parents feelings in a New York minute.

As a Family Therapist at a facility providing treatment to emotionally disturbed children I regularly scheduled monthly Family Fun nights. I served dinner because eating together is a bonding experience in families. I also planned some group activity such as pumpkin carving around

Halloween, decorating Christmas cookies, making Valentine's coupon books (good for 1 hug), etc. While it sounds so simple, teaching these families to play together was a very powerful experiential tool. Families in crisis have forgotten how to play and laugh together. As the family heals the chances of the child successfully overcoming their own difficulties are dramatically increased.

BUILDING AN UNDERSTANDING OF CHILDHOOD BEHAVIOR

There is a saying that goes: *When the student is ready, the teacher will appear.* So it goes with parenting and therapeutic interventions. It is the greatest exercise in humility, patience and love. We must listen and learn and to begin to see children as experts on childhood. To obtain an *accurate* picture of the child in their world. I place a lot of focus on treating the child holistically. I gather as much information about their life as I can. One helpful book that I have often used to help me see and understand where and how the child fits in their family I sometimes refer to Dr. Kevin Leman's book *The New Birth Order Book*. He speaks to the child's birth order position in the family and how it impacts the child and how they may see themselves and how others see them.

Even the most competent and confidant of people, in all walks of life, in all fields of work, find themselves challenged as never before once they add children to their lives.

One of the most helpful books I have read on this topic is Rudolf Dreikurs book "Children The Challenge". Although it was written many years ago, it remains relevant to this day. He explains much about not only what children do, but why. This thinking helps move the focus off the behavior alone and helps lead to understanding of what may be causing the behavior. Such understanding contributes much toward empowering parents to change the behavior of their children in a more positive direction rather than just "putting out fires". It also puts the child in more control over their own lives by using encouragement as opposed to punishment. Children usually respond to encouragement as opposed to praise. They also respond quicker to the use of natural and logical consequences rather than discipline. Consequences teach the child a better way to be while punishment is authoritarian and often leads to low self-esteem and shame. Logical consequences should be directly related to the behavioral infraction as much as possible and should be short lived. For example the use of time-outs should be, on average, 10 minutes per year of age, no longer. Grounding a child for a month not only requires constant vigilance by the parents, but by the time a month has passed the child has long ago forgotten what they did wrong.

Children know and understand much more about their own selves than we adults give them credit for. They are often much more competent than we realize. When we, as adults, get out of the way, we then have the opportunity to see just how able children really are. So whenever you are able, become an observer rather than automatically jumping in and taking over. Even in sibling quarrels when safety is not an issue. I worked with a mom who was having a lot of trouble with sibling quarrels. I asked her to stay out of it as much as she could and to wait and see what happened. During one fight between the youngest and smallest child and her older brother, Mom just observed. The little girl was resourceful and made up for the difference in size by grabbing a hairbrush as a weapon and evened the odds and ended the quarrel. By just staying out of it she learned just how capable and resourceful her little girl really was. And nobody got hurt. Children rarely actually intend to hurt one another. Most quarrels are for the parent's benefit.

By becoming an observer you are then more able to get an *accurate* view of the child. As mentioned before in a previous chapter I also rely on the works of Faber and Mazlich in their books *how To Talk So Children Will Listen and Listen So Children Will Talk, Without Spanking or Spoiling* and *Liberated Parents/Liberated Children*. The information gleaned form these three wonderful books has been incredibly helpful to me over the years. This information can be quite helpful in getting that all important accurate picture of the child.

Further, children are more responsive to nonverbal communication than are adults. They are extremely perceptive and absorb what goes on around them long before they can talk or even comprehend language. As mentioned previously the use of language is relatively new to young children. They still rely on nonverbal signals such as facial expressions, body positions and movement, eye movement or mood changes. They respond to bodily tension, increased heart rate and changes in breathing. They often recognize mood changes in adults before we are even aware we have those feelings. It's not easy to fool a child. Children are particularly affected by the way their parents, siblings and caregivers feel and act. They learn more rapidly horizontally than they do vertically in that they learn more quickly from their siblings and cohorts than from adults. Perhaps it's because they better understand one another.

Kids have their own particular form of communication and it does not often make much sense to adults. Faber and Mazlich and their book *"How To Talk So Kids Will Listen and Listen So kids Will Talk"*, has been a valuable resource for me and I often refer practitioners to it. They really have a well developed sense of how to best relate to children. I found this to be of particularly useful information when I was working as a forensic child interviewer. I had to be able to talk to the children on a level they could understand and accept and to get them to divulge their deepest, darkest secrets.

I always try my best to use the child's own words and stories when developing a treatment plan. I use the child's own language and descriptions of their discomfort or fears. When the child feels ownership of their problems they more readily become part of the solution.

KID SPEAK

I had a case with a 3 year old girl who was required to testify in court against her babysitter, a boy she really liked and was reluctant to talk about. Both the prosecuting and defense attorneys were having a great deal of difficulty communicating with her. She had been allowed to sit on her daddy's lap during her testimony and appeared to be quite comfortable and at ease. Not so with the attorneys. They frequently asked for 10 minute recesses wherein we would meet in the hallway and the attorneys would ask me how to ask questions to the little girl. This went on for awhile when she suddenly took ahold of the microphone and said to the prosecuting attorney, "Gil, would you like me to tell you what happened?" Gil responded affirmatively. She then proceeded to tell her story from beginning to end and then stated to her mother, "can I go to Burger King for French toast now?"

Developing the ability to communicate with young children on their level is imperative when doing therapeutic work with them. It is also imperative to have some knowledge of childhood development in order to determine normalcy and understanding their stories. Adults often fail to give credence to what children say. It has been my experience that when I meet them on their level I can readily and easily communicate with them about anything. By listening respectfully, and giving them my undivided attention, I am then able to identify the problem from their viewpoint and to work with them to find their own solution.

When I worked as a forensic child interviewer, interviewing young children who were suspected as being victims of physical or sexual abuse, I interviewed the child along with a detective from the jurisdictional agency. The detectives couldn't understand why the smaller kids would tell me everything about anything, but would not respond to and ignored the detectives. So I tried to help them understand how kids think and communicate. As per usual I referred them to Ms. Faber and Ms. Mazlich and their book *How to talk* . . . .

First of all it's a matter of how you look to the child. I routinely wore a Mickey Mouse t-shirt, funny earrings such as clowns, or my reliable Mickey Mouse watch that played "It's a small, small world" when I pushed the button. They, in turn, wore suits and ties and one even wore a handcuffs tie tack, and they had badges. It's not very child friendly. As luck would have it, one of the detectives had two young children of his own so I asked him how he related to them. Aha moment! He suddenly realized he often got down on the floor and wrestled and played with them which is much like the way I relate to children. I get down on the floor. I meet them on their level and I'm playful and friendly. Duh!! Thereafter, when we scheduled an interview with a young child, this detective lost the suit with the handcuffs tie clasp, the badge and even one time wore sweats and sat on the floor. This time the child talked to both of us. Lesson learned.

Having a good sense of humor, a willingness to be silly and to make a complete fool of yourself and to appear a bit bumbly goes a long way in relating to a young child. You try your best to appear much like what a child might create in their own imaginary ally in order to form an alliance with the child. First you have to earn their trust so they believe in you enough to share their story. Then perhaps you might be chosen to be a child's ally. It is quite an honor.

THROWING ROCKS

Tommy is a 4 year old very cute, bright, precocious little boy who was brought into my office by his mother due to his anger outbursts and the damages to the home and danger to the safety of others in the home. Tommy had a great right arm with a possible future in the MLB as a pitcher. Unfortunately, he was not throwing baseballs at a catcher's mitt, but rather rocks at windows. He liked the sound of the glass breaking and "tinkling" as it fell to the ground or floor. Of course this behavior was unacceptable and dangerous. It required quick attention.

I had to do a quick and dirty assessment and leave the fine details for later. Tommy was the youngest of 2 children having a sister 2 years older. Tommy was small for his age and his sister was normal height and weight for her age which made her even bigger than normally expected. She was also very cute, very bright and very precocious. At initial contact she looked like the perfect child. Very well mannered and friendly. Tommy, on the other hand, seemed a bit shy, avoided eye contact, and was not very communicative until you had gained his trust. I could only imagine what trying to compete with his sister for his mother's attention was like for him.

To add fuel to the fire Mom was involved in a lesbian relationship with a woman who was dealing with some very serious mental health issues which placed even further demands on Mom's time and attention. She had even less time to deal with Tommy, which in turn increased his acting out as he fought for his place in the family unit.

Unfortunately, Tommy's behavior escalated to the point he was placed in a psychiatric unit for 6 weeks after he cut his sister's face with glass shattered from a broken window.

However, this 6 week hiatus allowed me to focus more on what was going on within the family unit that contributed to Tommy's tantrums.

During this time Mom had more time to focus on the older sister. Without the focus being on Tommy's negative behaviors, Mom was able to see that the sister was not the perfect child she appeared to be without the contrast to Tommy.

When I work with families I develop and have all family members sign a "no hitting" contract. While there are often slip ups, generally speaking these contracts are very effective. At the very worst, the contract increases the awareness of the hitting that occurs between family members. I did so with Tommy's family as spanking was the primary mode of dealing with his tantrums and I felt it only further fed his anger.

There were no adult allies identified in Tommy's family as his grandparents lived some distance away. His relationship with them was solid and positive, but contact was minimal except for summer vacations. Tommy's father was absent from his life due to substance abuse issues. He had no relatives nearby. I had to get creative and quickly. There was also an ongoing custody battle in the court for custody of the children.

Tommy had very poor impulse control and by the time he thought about the possible consequences of his actions, he had already thrown the rock, or whatever. Because rocks were his weapon of choice I opted to look in that direction for an ally. Together we read Byrd Baylor's book "Everybody Needs a Rock" several times. Then we went on a couple of outings looking for "the" rock. As in the book, he got down on his hands and knees and "looked the rock in the eye". He touched them, tasted them. Held them to see if they felt smooth and soft in his hand. He pocketed them to see if they were "jumpy in his pocket" and we successfully found just the right rock. We washed and polished it until it was just right.

My instructions to him were to be sure he always had his rock in his pocket. In addition to the powers inherent in the rock we worked together to give the rock some additional "super powers". When he felt angry feelings or had angry thoughts he was to reach in his pocket for the rock. Tommy felt powerless, a victim of his own anger, but the rock's super powers enabled him, over time, to conquer his feelings of powerlessness and he gradually gained control over his anger. Sort of like how adults might use a "worry rock". Just feeling the rock, and knowing it was always there should he need it seemed to help Tommy. He never used his rock as a weapon.

During the course of this process I was able to ascertain that Tommy felt lost in his family; that he was not wanted and didn't belong. It became readily apparent that his goal driven behavior bounced around from attention, to power, but mainly in the realm of revenge. He felt hurt so he struck back in anger. He was determined to hurt others before they could hurt him. In addition I discovered Tommy had a real fear that he would be sent away to live with his father whom Tommy feared due to what occurred in the past due to his father's substance abuse. Tommy felt alone, afraid and powerless over any part of his life. He also feared his mother would leave him for her partner, choosing her over him, leaving him alone at the mercy of the court.

As mentioned previously, because troubled families often have difficulty having fun together I suggested various family outings that began slowly and improved in frequency and length over time. As I worked with the family to be more inclusive to Tommy and to be more inviting to him, his behavior began to improve. We found many more positive ways for him to find his place. Mom set aside time to devote solely to Tommy. He enjoyed his 1 on 1 time with her and would work to earn it.

Coupled with the sister being busted for her setting Tommy up we began making headway. We were replacing the bad with the good. Although I dislike Skinnerian theories, we were, in fact, extinguishing the behavior. The way Skinner describes his theoretical beliefs and the practices he uses to change targeted behavior seems cold, and disconnected to me. It's merely a matter of personal preference. It doesn't seem to matter much whose theories you subscribe too, only the words and methods change, but the results are much the same. You somehow reward the desired behavior and ignore the negative behavior to affect change. I instructed Mom to "catch" Tommy being good and recognizing his actions, such as "I saw you finished cleaning your room. You worked really hard". Not praise, but rather recognition of his efforts. Tommy's self esteem was low and he couldn't accept praise, but recognition? You betcha.

Once we got past Tommy's negative behaviors and got an accurate picture of what was really going on we began to address his anxieties and worries and his behavior miraculously improved. He was never angry at all, he was afraid. He wasn't either strawberry or raspberry jam. He wasn't jam at all, he was ketchup!

THE ANGRY CHILD

As I have mentioned previously in this book, it is difficult to determine Anxiety versus Attention Behavior Disorders. For this purpose I regularly administer the Achenbach CBCL to all adults in the child's life as each of them will see the child differently. This instruments assists me in gaining an *accurate* picture of the child from a variety of sources. This way I am also able to determine if there are any adult allies I can engage in therapy. Other therapists may use other resources to accomplish the same thing.

Because anger is always a secondary emotion, an anxious child might appear behaviorally like an angry child, particularly little boys. Or the anxiety is covered by the behavior, which results in a misdiagnosis and the treatment plan doesn't work well for the child. This becomes apparent in Rick and The Rocker and Throwing Rocks, both chapters in this book. Children who act out their feelings are often diagnosed with ADD/ADHD, Oppositional Defiant Disorder or Conduct Disorder. Some of the symptoms listed as diagnostic criteria are the same across the board for all four diagnoses. For example, the inability to concentrate on work or play is a symptom for both Anxiety Disorder and ADD/ADHD. This is, in part, why so many children are misdiagnosed as having ADD/ADHD, the most common diagnosis used for children.

In his book "The Angry Book", Theodore Isaac Rubin, M.D., says that children have the capacity to feel angry and to respond in some way at birth. Rubin states that infants who cry and scream and turn red with rage are responding to some increase in bodily tension, bodily discomfort or frustration. By contrast, referring to Carol Tavris' groundbreaking book (at least for its time): "Anger: The Misunderstood Emotion", she posits that anger begins to be expressed between the ages of 2 and 3. This comes as a big surprise to mothers. This is more in keeping with child developmental milestones. Children generally develop a sense of self at this age. Thus the angry expression is accepted as true emotion when in "the terrible twos". Tavris further states anger is *always a secondary emotion*. It is, therefore, critical to identify the primary emotion. Fear, hurt feelings, frustration are the biggies, but there are others. Rubin and Tavris are in agreement that anger has a primary emotional source. Anger is often an expression of anxiety or fear. It brings the child an instant sense of power and control while the fear/anxiety makes them feel helpless.

Anger is an incredibly useful tool according to Tavris. It brings instantaneous results. Anger is loud, threatening, demanding and almost always gets quick response. Children learn very early on to use this tool to meet their needs. Rubin believes that those of us who are physiologically whole are born with the potential to feel and express anger, but the particular ways in which we respond are not the same for everyone and is learned behavior, based primarily on the parental response to a child's expression of anger. Tavris disagrees that anger reactions are based solely on parental reaction and credits a plethora of information that forms one's angry response, including temperament.

At the risk of beating a dead horse, I once again wish to note that it is very difficult to discern the difference between an anxious child and a child with ADD/ADHD. Sometimes the only way doctors can tell is by prescribing certain medications. Like treating children much like lab rats. If this medication works then it must be X, if not it must be Y. Or maybe we need to try a different medication. I am not a supporter of the "shotgun" approach to treating children with medications and try to avoid the use of medication unless the behavior is way out of control and stronger methods need to be applied. That is purely my opinion and I am sure many will disagree and that's okay.

REAL FEARS

Not all fears are imagined or irrational. As stated prior in this book, fear is a natural reaction to an event. Anxiety is an irrational reaction to what *might* happen. This natural reaction then leads to Anxiety Disorders, Post Traumatic Stress Disorder and can feed Anger problems. Treating anxiety related to an actual event is more difficult in some ways than those that are imagined. In either case, real or imagined, the irrationality of the anxiety remains the same. The difficulty in dealing with real events is the possibility of the event reoccurring is just as real as the initial event. So the *might happen* is much more powerful.

However, many of the same techniques used with imaginary fears can also be used in reality based anxiety. After the basic intake procedures have been completed, I begin to look for allies. As in all the cases mentioned in this book, allies can be real or imagined, determined, in part, by the age of the child. If the child is under the age of 5, and no living and real allies can be found, I begin to work with the child to create an imaginary friend.

I prefer to use a real, live person as an ally in reality based anxiety if one can be found because the trust bond between the child and their special person is inherently much stronger. Plus the trust all ready exists which saves time and energy to create an ally. Ideally, the person the child identifies would be a parent, because of the close proximity. Grandparents, aunts and uncles also make good allies, but are not always present. For example, the child may only see their grandparents on the weekends.

Anxieties severe enough to drive parents to bring their child into your office for treatments have already disrupted the family structure and may have damaged the parent-child relationship. The parents are always at their wits end. That's why they're in your office. If they could find a way to handle the situation on their own they already would have.

Usually the parents I meet are sleep deprived, frustrated beyond their ability to cope and feel as though they have somehow failed as a parent. Therefore, some work must begin as soon as possible to encourage, support and reinforce the parents and to repair any damage done to the relationship with their child. Once parents begin to understand what's happening with their child and are given support and new skills to try, they become increasingly empowered and, therefore, a stronger ally for the child.

Very often the parents have lost their patience with the child and may have reacted to the child's irrational behavior in anger, which is brought on by their feelings of frustration and failure. But angry responses further instill the fear and anxiety in the child. Many times I schedule separate appointments for the parent(s) and the child and I make sure the child is aware of these appointments. I refer to them as Mommy/Daddy school where parents learn new tricks to "battle" the child's fears. In reality what happens during these appointments is that I refer parents to parenting classes/groups if there are some available in the community, introduce them to books I have found to be helpful or any other available resource to help them learn to cope with the problems they are experiencing.

Additionally, I try and find ways to get some respite for the parent(s) so they can get some sleep, relax and regroup. The stronger the parent, the stronger the ally. And in these cases I need a really strong ally for the child.

HOME BY NOON

I was assigned to work with a 7 year old second grade boy who was part of a wrap around program through the county mental health agency where I was working at the time. I went to the school and met with the school principal who was asking that the boy be sent home each day at noon. I explained to him that under Federal Law guidelines that was not a possibility and we had to find another answer.

At the time I came to the case this boy had stabbed another student in the head with a pencil, had injured another child with scissors and had repeatedly physically attacked other students and school staff. He was in the classroom 10% of the time and in the Resource Room 90% of his school day. I began the search for an ally for this boy.

The parent-child relationship was strained to the max. His grandfather was estranged from the boy. There was no father in the picture. His relationships at school and in the community were strained. He was too old for the use of imaginary friends as he was developed well into the stage of critical and linear thinking. And he virtually trusted no one.

I met with the Director of the agency and we decided to use some of the funds assigned to the wrap around program to hire a "shadow" for him while at school. I interviewed, hired and trained a wonderful woman whose task it was to meet this boy at the door in the morning and to stay with him throughout the school day and to walk him to the bus at the end of the day. I trained her in the use of soft, positive restraint techniques and together we went to work to resolve this child's issues.

This woman worked very closely with the boy, often mopping up the floor while restraining him in the school hallway. But, gradually over time she began to earn his trust. Over the first year we were able to maintain him through the school day with no further attacks. He began to see his "shadow" as his "ally". He knew he could rely on her to keep him safe even when he was out of control himself. But troubles continued at home and in the community.

Thankfully, we were able to get the funding to keep his "shadow" over the summer vacation months and got the boy involved in team sports and several summer activity programs. She took him to the grocery store, the library, the bank and to restaurants. She taught him both by her example and by explanation the appropriate way to behave in the community and he gradually began to make friends and earn some trust in the community which had a dramatic effect on his behavior. He made a few friends on his sports teams and was learning how to appropriately make friends.

By the end of the second year of working with him he was in the regular classroom 90% of the time and in the Resource Room 10% of his school day. I believe his success was due directly to the creation of an ally with the use of his "shadow". With her constant and consistent support he had success, after success after success until it became the norm for him. His relationship with his mother improved some, but they continued to struggle due to her own difficulties. However, his relationship with his Grandfather dramatically improved. He and his grandfather went on fishing trips together and Grandpa attended all of his baseball and soccer games. When we gradually pulled the support from the "shadow" he transferred his alliance and trust to the grandfather.

Over the course of treatment I was able to ascertain the contributing primary emotion feeding his angry outbursts was anxiety resulting from his mother's substance abuse difficulties. His world and life was one of total uncertainty. The more he acted out in his fear the more he drove people away from him which, in turn, increased his fear. As he was able to learn trust and safety beginning at school and moving out into the community, he needed his anger less and less. He used his anger as a tool to keep others at bay because of his mistrust. Through the treatment program we were able to create for him, he was able to break out of the vicious cycle of fear and defense into having normal, trusting relationships with others, particularly with his peers. The principal who initially just wanted to get rid of him was now greeting him at the door each morning with a smile and a welcoming handshake or hug.

I believe this case has had more personal impact on me as a person and as a professional more than any other because the outcome was so dramatically successful. It is incredibly empowering to watch a child literally turn their life around from almost total failure to almost total success. Although he was given lots of support, encouragement and protection, he still had to make the turn around in his life choices himself. He worked really hard once he began to experience the feeling of having some success in his life. He had a lot to overcome and he did it and the last I heard about him his success has continued. And I think it is important to note that the outcome was HIS success not mine. All I did was find him an ally. He took the ball and ran with it.

RICKY AND THE ROCKER

While working as the Family Therapist at a residential treatment center for emotionally disturbed children I had the joyful experience of being selected by a child to serve as his ally. I had a large, oak rocking chair in my office and all the children knew it was there.

One day this boy came to my door and asked me if I would rock him. Since he was pushing 12 his size made it a bit difficult but together we found a way to make it work.

This young man came into the center with the diagnosis of Oppositional Defiant Disorder. He had a horrendous history of abuse and neglect. His behavior was way out of control.

He had no contact with his family and lived in a group home. He had great difficulty using words to communicate his needs rather he would act out and thereby get attention. When a child was out of control and posed a danger to themselves, or others, the staff would implement the use of soft restraint. Over time it became apparent that this boy acted out in order to get staff members to hold him. Because of his difficulty verbalizing his needs his request came as a bit of a surprise.

So we agreed that one day per week I would rock him in my rocking chair. When I rocked him I usually sang silly songs such as "Old McDonald Had A Farm" and others that I routinely sang to my own children and grandchildren. He sucked it up. His behavior began to improve. The children were able to earn "points" for their good behavior. We had a "school store" with items kids liked or they could save their points and spend them as cash at a local store and this boy rarely had any points to spend. I distinctly remember how proud he was when he got to cash in his first points. Whatever was happening for him in that rocking chair seemed to help. I believe I was reparenting him, fulfilling a long denied need for affection in a safe way. The changes in his behavior were nothing short of miraculous. His plan was working for him.

Recognizing his new found success with the rocking chair I developed a "coupon book" with coupons he could cash in with staff members who also became his allies. The first people he found he could trust and felt safe with. He had coupons good for 1 hug, or 5-10 minutes 1 on 1 time, or to go for a walk, etc. We used the coupons for a relatively short period of time until he became able to verbally request his need for the first time in his life. He was learning to trust, not just in others, but in himself. He was learning to self-soothe. Tools that were robbed from him by all the years of abuse and neglect.

I was proud to have been chosen by him to be his first ally and to watch him grow in trust and confidence. It was not due to any action on my part. And it certainly was not due to my wonderful singing voice. I can't carry a tune in a box. For some reason he seemed to believe I was a safe person and that was how I was chosen. That and the magical rocking chair. I think it was that chair. It was his deal and his alone. He had found a way on his own to help relieve him of his anxieties and worries. It was his plan and because he owned it he was greatly empowered by a simple rocking chair and some silly songs.

REBUILDING TRUST

Because the child may have lost some or all of the trust they once had in others, even their parents, I do some trust building exercises to rebuild or repair that bond. And because the child's behavior has become so disruptive to the family as a whole, family activities that were once enjoyable have often fallen by the wayside because the parents time is being consumed by a child who is out of control in some way or another. Sometimes I will advise family outings or activities without the identified client. To avoid any hurt feelings I suggest engaging the anxious child in some special activity they particularly enjoy, such as a day with Grandma, so they see this time as special and avoids feelings of exclusion. Families who have a child with emotional and behavioral difficulties have often forgotten how to have fun. So I try to teach them to get creative in order to rebuild their lives and restore the family order.

Siblings can make excellent allies as well. Actually, sometimes even better than a parent because they often enjoy similar activities and they communicate with one another more on a lateral level. Plus kids are usually more creative with active imaginations, have more energy and aren't sleep deprived, hopefully.

So by looking at the child as a whole, not just as an individual, trying to see life through their eyes 24/7, you may be able to identify and strengthen an allegiance bond with someone in the family. If not, it's back to magic 101 and creating an imaginary friend who's given super powers and magic to defeat the offending fearful event/object.

THE CASE OF THE TIPSY TV

A young mother brought her 4 year old daughter in to my office because she was having a great deal of difficulty dealing with her daughter's fear of their television set. As it so happened, one day the girl was running in the house and accidentally bumped the stand the tv sat on and it tipped over and fell on the floor narrowly missing the little girl.

Since then Susie has refused to be alone anywhere in the house, following her Mom from room to room constantly, giving the poor Mom no room to breathe and worst of all, no privacy. This behavior worsened when in any proximity to the offending television, which was near the doorway between the living room and the kitchen. In order for Susie to navigate between the two rooms she had to hold onto her mother. As Mom described it, "she literally clings to me so tight I can barely walk, wrapping herself around me". To make matters even worse Susie had begun having nightmares and demanded to sleep in her mother's bed.

Susie and her mother lived with her maternal grandmother, who Susie dearly loved. Susie loved and trusted both her mother and her grandmother, both of whom were present in the home all day, except when Susie went to preschool for 3 hours, from 9 a.m. until noon which was the only break the Mom had.

It appeared as if both mother and grandmother could serve as an ally for Susie in dealing with the tipsy tv. Because the mother was kept so busy dealing with Susie's behavior I opted to try Grandma as the ally. I searched for some books with similar stories that I could read with Susie. Looking for books that might have a grandparent as a hero of sorts. I even made up some such stories giving grandparents special powers. Grandma willingly agreed to play the part of the heroine of the play. First, she and Susie went shopping for a special piece of furniture the television could sit on more safely. It had to be quite sturdy to make sure the tv would not fall ever again. Just as in finding a "special" rock, it had to be "just right". And it had some super powers to keep the tv under control at all times. Then Grandma moved the tv to a much better location, subject to Susie's approval. Involving Susie directly in solving the problem empowered her to the point that the nightmares began to fall away as did Susie's clinging to her mother. Susie still wanted to be in the same room as her Mom, but it was beginning to get better in the household for a 3 of them.

Next, Grandma and Susie went shopping for just the right thing to tie the tv onto the stand to further ensure it would never fall off again. They purchased a bright red bungie cord at the local hardware store, brought it home and installed it securely over the television and hooking onto 2 handles on the stand. Grandma and Susie stood back and admired their good work. Grandma gave an academy award winning performance as she looked closely at the cord from every angle with lots of "oohs" and "ahs" and "mmm-hmms". "Yep", she said, "I think we did it". Surprisingly, Susie agreed. Over the next few weeks Susie stopped clinging to her mother and the nightmares disappeared. It appeared peace had been restored to the household. Susie actually asked to watch cartoons, which she had not done for several months since the fall of the television.

Grandma had been a great ally for Susie. By involving Susie actively and closely empowered Susie. Her self-esteem improved greatly. She became her happy self once more. As Susie's feelings about herself got stronger she was once again able to self soothe relying less and less on others for comfort. I forgot to mention Grandma had sewn Susie a special doll with magical powers sewn inside in the form of crystals, tucked inside a small drawstring bag, that "stood guard" over Susie as she slept. The doll became the anti-nightmare ally. So with a lot of grandmotherly love and creativity, plus a doll with magical powers sewn inside another successful conclusion was reached.

REAL FEARS

Not all fears are imagined or irrational. As stated prior in this book, fear is a natural reaction to an event. Anxiety is an irrational reaction to what *might* happen. This natural reaction then leads to Anxiety Disorders, Post Traumatic Stress Disorder and can feed Anger problems. Treating anxiety related to an actual event is more difficult in some ways than those that are imagined. In either case, real or imagined, the irrationality of the anxiety remains the same. The difficulty in dealing with real events is the possibility of the event reoccurring is just as real as the initial event. So the *might happen* is much more powerful.

However, many of the same techniques used with imaginary fears can also be used in reality based anxiety. After the basic intake procedures have been completed, I begin to look for allies. As in all the cases mentioned in this book, allies can be real or imagined, determined, in part, by the age of the child. If the child is under the age of 5, and no living and real allies can be found, I begin to work with the child to create an imaginary friend.

I prefer to use a real, live person as an ally in reality based anxiety if one can be found because the trust bond between the child and their special person is inherently much stronger. Plus the trust all ready exists which saves time and energy to create an ally. Ideally, the person the child identifies would be a parent, because of the close proximity. Grandparents, aunts and uncles also make good allies, but are not always present. For example, the child may only see their grandparents on the weekends.

Anxieties severe enough to drive parents to bring their child into your office for treatments have already disrupted the family structure and may have damaged the parent-child relationship. The parents are always at their wits end. That's why they're in your office. If they could find a way to handle the situation on their own they already would have.

Usually the parents I meet are sleep deprived, frustrated beyond their ability to cope and feel as though they have somehow failed as a parent. Therefore, some work must begin as soon as possible to encourage, support and reinforce the parents and to repair any damage done to the relationship with their child. Once parents begin to understand what's happening with their child and are given support and new skills to try, they become increasingly empowered and, therefore, a stronger ally for the child.

Very often the parents have lost their patience with the child and may have reacted to the child's irrational behavior in anger, which is brought on by their feelings of frustration and failure. But angry responses further instill the fear and anxiety in the child. Many times I schedule separate appointments for the parent(s) and the child and I make sure the child is aware of these appointments. I refer to them as Mommy/Daddy school where parents learn new tricks to "battle" the child's fears. In reality what happens during these appointments is that I refer parents to parenting classes/groups if there are some available in the community, introduce them to books I have found to be helpful or any other available resource to help them learn to cope with the problems they are experiencing.

Additionally, I try and find ways to get some respite for the parent(s) so they can get some sleep, relax and regroup. The stronger the parent the stronger the ally. And in these cases I need a really strong ally for the child.

GRIEF AND LOSS

Loss of people, pets; those we care about and love is a normal part of the circle of life. But, for a young child, such losses can be overwhelming and can lead to an Anxiety Disorder severe enough to require professional intervention. Young children lack an understanding of death which puts them at risk for anxiety reactions to the reality of their loss. The what "*might*" happen can feed into their fears. Most of the time, with support, love and understanding, children can overcome their sense of grief and loss. If not, you will see them in your office.

I have had some success, not necessarily with the direct use of allies, but with stories and other activities that fall into the realm of conventional (allopathic) play therapy with the specific theme of grief and loss. One of my favorite books on this subject is "*Koko's Kitten*" the story of a gorilla who loses her kitten. Children can often identify with an animal when they can't with another person. Another favorite animal story of mine is "*The Tenth Best Thing About Barney*". It is a story about a boy who loses his dog. I have also watched the movie "*The Lion King*" with a child and then talked with them about the "great circle of life".

In addition to reading books, watching movies and acting out their feelings through play, I often recommend the child join a group for children suffering from grief and loss if there is one in the community. If there is not one available I encourage parents to start one. Because children learn quicker laterally, from one another, this can be an effective tool for the therapist in assisting the child and family.

In keeping with the theme of this book, I do look for allies within the child's world, whether real or imagined. As in all cases of fear and anxiety such allies can be powerful tools to assist the child and lead to a successful, positive outcome to relieve the child's anxieties around death, dying and illness. Remember there is a difference between fear and anxiety. Anxiety results from the *what if,* the belief it can happen again even if it probably won't.

It is also important to remember and understand the stages of the grieving process and often refer to Elizabeth Kubler Ross's book "*On Death And Dying*". This can also be helpful to the parents. I also often refer the parents to join their own grief group to help deal with their own feelings of grief and loss. Again, the more you empower the parent, the better the chance they can in turn help their child. The stages of grief are much the same for children as they are in adults. Understanding what stage they might be in gives a better opportunity to help them cope. Because the stages of grief are different for each individual, and do not occur in a specific order, the child may be in a different stage of the grieving process than the parent. This can impact the normal healing process for both, but it can also become a useful tool as in "I remember when I felt that way and this is what I did to feel better . . . ."

Understanding the grieving process and being in control of your own feelings of loss and sadness can greatly reduce the chances of an Anxiety Disorder forming in a child. Of course it is perfectly normal to display feelings of sadness and loss incase of death, loss or serious illness in the family, dealing with your own grief or concern give children a better chance of coming through the process unscathed. Remember children are excellent listeners but lousy interpreters and they may misconstrue your feelings of grief and loss.

TIPS FOR PARENTS

Coping with a child with an Anxiety Disorder is trying at least. Having a child period is a trial. I love the quote "you can't scare me I have children". Oprah Winfrey has said many times that she feels parenting is the most important, and the toughest, job there is. I agree. So I've added a few tips on parenting that I have found to be helpful for me.

In Dinkmeyer & Mc Cays book, "S.T.E.P.: The Systematic Training For Effective Parenting they discuss four basic goals of child behavior: Attention, Power, Revenge and Assumed Disability. Assumed Disability is so rarely seen I tend to disregard it. According to this book, children's behavior is driven by an unconscious goal. Being able to look at the goal(s) of the behavior allows you to take a step back from focusing only on the behavior itself and to look more closely at what might be driving the behavior. Parents are so busy putting out the forest fires they end up spinning their wheels and getting nowhere. Understanding the underlying cause of their behavior allows parents a whole new way for longer lasting intervention. This information has worked well for me.

While a student I spent several years in various positions at a child/parent center learning and teaching the concept of goal directed behavior to other parents and students. I have also used this model as a Family Therapist. I often describe Attention using the analogy of a mosquito. The mosquito buzzes by your ear and you swat at it only to have it return time and time again. You feel irritated. With Power a parent feels their authority is challenged and they often think/feel "I'll teach you whose boss". If you are in a power struggle with a child you have already lost and you may as well just give up for the moment and revisit the issue later. Kids have way more free brain power than adults do. It is much better to try and give the child as much power over their own life as they are able. For instance, giving them a choice of what to wear or what to have for dinner. However, you need to limit the choice to 2 or 3 or you could be there all day or night. With Revenge the parent feels hurt by the child's actions and might think "how could you do this to me"? For whatever reason the child feels hurt and strikes out to hurt others. I highly recommend this book to all the parents I have worked with and continue to recommend it to any parent having difficulty with their children.

This and the many other parenting books now available can help parents to discipline their children in the same manner. There are also parenting classes available in nearly every town in the USA. As mentioned earlier in this book parents who discipline their children in very different styles may create an Anxiety Disorder in their child and no parent I know of would want that. When I was raising my children in the late '60's and 70's there was not the plethora of information available to me and children do not arrive with a set of instructions tattooed on their butts so I was parenting by the seat of my pants. So take advantage of whatever information suits you and your family the best.

Parents can actively participate in the treatment process and things always go more smoothly when they do. This is in keeping with treating the child holistically. There are a number of specific things parents can do to relieve their child's anxiety that may be feeding their anger:

- Encourage the child to talk about their feelings. To use their words as opposed to acting out their feelings.
- Consistently reassure and comfort the child. Without overly reacting to the fear/anxiety, but assuring the child of their belonging and place in the family unit reduces their anxious feelings.
- Teach your child relaxation techniques such as deep breathing, counting to 10 and use of self talk. The child has lost their ability to self soothe so teaching them these specific techniques allows them to return to the normal self soothing they once had.
- Maintain routines as much as possible, discuss changes in advance to avoid surprises. Routine allows the child the "brain room" to focus on what's making them afraid without having to worry about what "*might*" happen next, because they already know. Change is uncomfortable for an anxious child because they fear the unknown in addition to their irrational fear that's causing their current problems. The more a parent can do to explain and prepare the child for the change, the easier the transition will be. For example, visiting the new pre-school before their first day.

- Remind the child often about past successes they have had. Before anxiety reared it's ugly head, children have usually been able to cope with life as a whole and to self soothe. Once they're in the throes of their fears they forget they once knew how to cope. Helping them remember their past successes reassures them they can do it again.
- Do not accommodate the child's fears. Keep it business as usual. Over reacting to the child's fears actually feeds the anxiety. The calmer the parent, the calmer the child. While it's important to acknowledge the child's fear as being real to them, treating it as a reality makes it worse, not better.
- Watch out for your own fears and anxieties that might be contributing to their child's difficulties. In some cases, the parent might share the same fear the child has, such as a fear of heights. It's important to help the parents cope with their own feelings of anxiety so they don't over react to the child's anxiety. There have been cases where I have referred the parent to therapy to help them in this process. They cannot help their child if they too are frozen in fear.

INTERNET RESOURCES

www.childanxiety.net

www.keepkidshealthy.com

www.a4pt

RESOURCES FOR KIDS

Baylor, Byrd: *Everybody Needs A Rock*; Athenium Books, New York (1974)

Baylor, Byrd: *The Other Way To Listen*; Charles Scribner's Sons, New York (1978)

Holmes, Margaret: *A Terrible Thing Happened*

Lobby, Ted: *Jessica and the Wolf: A Story of Children Who Have Bad Dreams.* *de*Brunhoff, Laurent: *Babar's Yoga For Elephants*

Grief and loss:

Patterson, Dr. Francine: *Koko's Kitten;* Scholastic, Inc., New York (1985)

Sheppard, Caroline: *Brave Bart: A Story for Traumatized and Grieving Children*

The 10ᵗʰ Best Thing About Barney

Separation Anxiety:

Brown, Marc: *Arthur Goes To Camp;* Econ-Clad Books, (1999)

Jeram, Anita; *Bunny, My Honey:* Candlewick Press, (2001)

Alexander, Liza: *Ernie Gets Lost:* Western (1998)

Nethery, Mary: *Hannah and Jack;* Atheneum, (1996)

Fitzpatrick, Marie-Louise: *Lizzy and Skunk:* Dorling Kindersley (2000)

Kandoian, Ellen: *Maybe She Forgot:* Penguin (1990)

Senderak, Carol: *Mommy In My Pocket:* Hyperion (2006)

Waddell, Martin: *Owl Babies:* Candlewick (1996)

Howe, James: *Pinky and Rex Go To Camp;* Macmillan (1992)

Hendry, Diana: *Very Noisy Night:* Puffin Books (2001)

Maier, Inger & Candon, Jennifer: *When Fuzzy Was Afraid Of Losing His Mother:* Magination Press (2005)

Kraus, Robert: *Whose Mouse Are You?:* Simon and Schuster (2000)

Corey, Dorothy: *You Go Away:* A. Whitman and Co. (1999)

Ages 8-12

Crist, James: *What To Do When You're Scared and Worried:* Free Spirit (2004)

RESOURCES FOR PARENTS

Brown, Jeffrey L. : *No More Monsters In The Closet: Teaching your Children to Overcome Everyday Fears and Phobias*; Crown Publishing,(1995)

Chansky, Tamar: *Freeing Your Child From Anxiety: Powerful, Practical Solutions to Overcome Your Child's Fears, Worries and Phobias*; Broadway Books, (2004)

Dinkmeyer & McCay: *S.T.E.P.: The Systematic Training for Effective Parenting.* Circle Pines, MN (1997)

Eisen, Andrew: *Helping Your Child Overcome Separation Anxiety or School Refusal: a Step-by-Step Guide for Parents*; New Harbinger Publishing, (2006)

Last, Cynthia: *Help For Worried Kids: How Your Child Can Conquer Anxiety and Fear*; Guilford Press, (2006)

Wagner, Aureen Pinto, PhD: *Worried No More: Help and Hope for Anxious Children.* Lighthouse Press.

BIBLIOGRAPHY

Achenbach, Thomas: *The Child Behavior Check List*; University of Vermont.

Diagnostic And Statistical Manual For Mental Disorders, 4th Edition, Text Revision, (DSM IV TR): American Psychiatric Association (2000).

Dinkmeyer & McCay; *S.T.E.P: The Systematic Training For Effective Parenting*; Circle Pines, MN (1997)

Kirkpatrick, Jane: *A Sweetness To The Soul*; Multnomah books, (1995)

Leman, Kevin: *The New Birth Order Book*; Baker Book House Company, Grand Rapids, MI (1999)

Faber, Adele & Mazlich, Elaine *How To Talk So Children Will Listen And Listen So Kids Will Talk*: First Avon Books, NY (1999); *Without Spanking or Spoiling*: Avon Books, NY (); and *Liberated parents, Liberated Children*: Avon Books (1990)

Rubin, Theodore Isaac, M.D.; *The Angry Book*; Collier Books, New York (1969)

Tavris, Carol : *Anger: The Misunderstood Emotion*: Simon & Schuster, Inc., New York (1982)

ABOUT THE AUTHOR

Sandra Nelson, MA, NCC attended Lane Community College for 2 years majoring in Liberal Arts and Psychology. She graduated from the University of Oregon with a Bachelor of Arts Degree in Developmental Psychology and a Master of Arts Degree in Counseling. She is a Nationally Certified Counselor. She has worked as a Family Therapist, a Child and Family Specialist and a Forensic Child Interviewer.

She has worked in the field of Child and Family Mental Health for over 20 years and has attended numerous post-graduate trainings, seminars and workshops.

She developed the model of using allies in the treatment of children with Anxiety Disorders early on in her career. She has shared the use of this treatment concept with coworkers, friends, family, and other professionals working in the field. The use of allies as a treatment tool has successfully been replicated by others.

Sandy worked in a residential treatment facility for emotionally disturbed children from the ages of 3 to 12 years as a Family Therapist.

While working as a Child/Family Specialist at a County Mental Health Center in Washington State she gained some local recognition for her work using children's magical thinking as a therapeutic tool, working primarily with young children from the ages of 3 to 6. She has been known for her ability to work with such young children both as a therapist and a forensic interviewer.

Sandy worked in a Child Advocacy Center as a Forensic Child Interviewer working with multi-agency law enforcement interviewing children suspected as being victims of abuse.

In her personal life Sandy is the mother of four boys, now adults. She is the grandmother of 7, all boys except for one little granddaughter, whose ages range from 22 to 2. She and her husband had a therapeutic foster home for over 5 years with 4 permanent children. There was always a steady stream of kids in and out of the house.

Sandy is currently retired and lives with her husband in Eugene, Oregon. She has volunteered for several agencies dealing with women's and children's issues. She remains an active advocate for children and families.

www.ingramcontent.com/pod-product-compliance
Lightning Source LLC
Chambersburg PA
CBHW030402290526
45785CB00004B/1864